LION BRAND YARN

JUST**WRAPS**

Also by Lion Brand Yarn
Lion Brand Yarn: Just Hats
Lion Brand Yarn: Just Scarves
Lion Brand Yarn: Just Bags
Lion Brand Yarn: Vintage Styles for Today

LION BRAND YARN

JUST**WRAPS**

30 PATTERNS TO KNIT AND CROCHET

EDITED BY STEPHANIE KLOSE AND CATHY MAGUIRE

POTTER
CRAFT

NEW YORK

The authors and publisher would like to thank the Craft Yarn
Council of America for providing the yarn weight standards
and accompanying icons used in this book. For more
information, please visit www.YarnStandards.com.

Published in the United States by Potter Craft,
an imprint of the Crown Publishing Group,
a division of Random House, Inc.

POTTER CRAFT and CLARKSON N. POTTER are trademarks
and POTTER and colophon are registered trademarks of
Random House, Inc.

Printed in Singapore

Design by Caitlin Daniels Israel
Editors: Stephanie Klose and Cathy Maguire
Photography: Jack Deutsch

Library of Congress Cataloging-in-Publication

ISBN: 0-307-20992-X

10 9 8 7 6 5 4 3 2 1

First Edition

CONTENTS

INTRODUCTION

Wraps come in numerous shapes and styles, including boas, capes, capelets, ponchos, rebozos, serapes, shawls, shrugs, and stoles. Universal and embracing, wraps have been made around the world for centuries. In terms of style, wraps have more to offer than the simple scarf but provide the same ease and comfort of a garment free of sleeves and complicated tailoring.

Just Wraps celebrates this most versatile garment and presents both knit and crochet patterns that include a classic men's poncho, or "moncho," inspired by the colorful serapes worn by men in Mexico, a kimono-like shrug made from a microfiber yarn that drapes like silk, and an adorable child's poncho embellished with simple embroidery. Easy-to-follow knit and crochet instructions are accompanied by directions for specialized construction methods for flat and circular knitting. Multicolored yarns that range from fine to super bulky are knit, crocheted, and embroidered to produce an array of new and interesting textures. A whole host of color and yarn textures range from soft yarns to glitzy yarns, as well as classic staples. Whether your style is vintage or modern, traditional or contemporary, you'll find our wraps hard to resist.

There are seven chapters in this book, each with a specific focus. Each chapter gradually introduces new skills and tips that clarify the many operations that go into the construction of a successful wrap. Beginners will want to start with the easy patterns in chapter one (which include simple instructions for pieced knitting) and work their way up to the later chapters that cover more specialized knitting and crocheting techniques such as cable knitting (chapter 3), and intarsia knitting, granny squares, and Fair Isle knitting (chapter 4). Each chapter features fashionable and functional projects that reinforce your newly learned skills. However, there are easy patterns included in every single chapter, so if you know the basics, feel free to jump from chapter to chapter.

This book assumes that if you knit you know how to knit and purl and if you crochet that you can single crochet, double crochet, and half double crochet. If you need to learn or refresh your memory about these basic stitches, there are a number of free resources. Learntoknit.com, learntocrochet.com, and lionbrand.com offer good introductions to first-time stitchers. Crochet.about.com and knitting.about.com provide tutorials on more advanced techniques as well as forums for asking questions of the experts on staff.

Most libraries have basic knitting and crochet reference books and knitting and crochet guilds welcome new members. Knitters and crocheters are making their presence felt in public, on subways and buses. Knitting ambassadors are preaching to the converted world of Hollywood starlets and ex-con business tycoons. Stitchers are everywhere; you only have to seek to find a few friends familiar with needles and hooks. Ask around for local groups who organize "knit and network" meetings at coffee shops or for "stitch and bitch" groups you can join.

We have followed the standards and guidelines created by the Craft Yarn Council of America to help you choose patterns that are right for your skill level. Each pattern is labeled as Beginner, Easy, Intermediate, or Experienced. **Beginner** patterns are suitable for first-time knitters and crocheters and only require basic stitch skills. **Easy** patterns call for basic stitches, repetitive pattern work, simple color changes, simple shaping, and finishing. Intermediate patterns include a variety of techniques (such as lacework, simple intarsia, double-pointed needles, and finishing). Projects using more complicated techniques—such as short rows, multicolor changes, complicated cables, lace patterns, fine threads, small needles and hooks, and detailed shaping and finishing—are for experienced knitters and crocheters.

CHOOSING YOUR YARN

Wraps can be made with just about any yarn, but give special consideration to the season in which you

STANDARD YARN WEIGHT SYSTEM

YARN WEIGHT SYMBOL & CATEGORY NAMES	1 SUPER FINE	2 FINE	3 LIGHT	4 MEDIUM	5 BULKY	6 SUPER BULKY
TYPE OF YARNS IN CATEGORY	Sock, Fingering, Baby	Sport, Baby	DK, Light Worsted	Worsted, Afghan, Aran	Chunky, Craft, Rug	Bulky, Roving
KNIT GAUGE RANGE* IN STOCKINETTE STITCH TO 4 INCHES	27–32 sts	23–26 sts	21–24 sts	16–20 sts	12–15 sts	6–11 sts
RECOMMENDED NEEDLE IN METRIC SIZE RANGE	2.25–3.25 mm	3.25–3.75 mm	3.75–4.5 mm	4.5–5.5 mm	5.5–8 mm	8 mm and larger
RECOMMENDED NEEDLE IN U.S. SIZE RANGE	1 to 3	3 to 5	5 to 7	7 to 9	9 to 11	11 and larger
CROCHET GAUGE RANGES* IN SINGLE CROCHET TO 4 INCHES	21–32 sts	16–20 sts	12–17 sts	11–14 sts	8–11 sts	5–9 sts
RECOMMENDED HOOK IN METRIC SIZE RANGE	2.25–3.5 mm	3.5–4.5 mm	4.5–5.5 mm	5.5–6.5 mm	6.5–9 mm	9 mm and larger
RECOMMENDED HOOK IN U.S. SIZE RANGE	B–1 to E–4	E–4 to 7	7 to I–9	I–9 to K–10½	K–10½ to M–13	M–13 and larger

*Guidelines only: The above reflect the most commonly used gauges and needle or hook sizes for specific yarn categories.

intend to wear the project. Wool and wool blends, acrylics, and chenilles work wonderfully for fall/winter wraps and ponchos. Cotton and cotton blends, microfiber yarns, and ribbon yarns are more suitable for spring/summer wraps. Fur and metallic yarns are excellent for year-round evening wraps. Loose, lacy gauge works best for spring/summer and a tighter gauge for fall/winter items.

There are several important things to keep in mind when making wraps for children. First, choose your yarn wisely. Who hasn't heard a child complain about a sweater being "too itchy"? Make sure the yarn is soft enough for sensitive young skin. Look for yarns that are machine washable. Wool blends, acrylics, and some novelty yarns are great choices.

In today's marketplace there is a dazzling array of yarns. Knowing the inherent qualities of each type of yarn will lead you to pleasing results when you experiment with different texture combinations. Traditional smooth yarns give good stitch definition and are great for trying different stitches or experimenting with color. Available in a variety of gauges from super fine to extra bulky, these yarns also come in a wide range of fibers and blends to fit any project or budget.

Brushed yarns produce a "halo" of hairlike fibers and work well on large needles and hooks in simple stitches. They include mohair, mohair blends, angora, and synthetic yarns that imitate the brushed look. Chenille yarn looks and feels like velvet. It is best to knit and crochet this yarn at a firm gauge.

Other yarns are heavily textured. Bouclés, for instance, are "loopy" yarns, which can help to hide a multitude of stitching sins. They are best used on

larger needles and hooks. One caution: Make sure to pick up the entire thread and not to catch your needle or hook on the "loop" part on the yarn only. Eyelash or fur yarns make great accents or can be used for complete projects. Since the "lash" part of the yarn is often connected by a thin thread, eyelash yarns can easily be worked with other yarns to produce subtly sensational effects. Try combining two different colors of eyelash to create a mélange of colors. A good rule of thumb with any fancy or textured yarn is "less is more." Save the fancy stitchwork for smooth yarns that will show your hard work to full advantage. Let the dazzling yarn do the work for you.

SUBSTITUTING YARN

When describing yarn, terms like "bulky" or "sport-weight" can mean different things to different people. The Craft Yarn Council of America has established guidelines called the Standard Yarn Weight System to standardize descriptions of yarn thickness (see page 9). The materials section of each pattern in this book features an icon of a skein of yarn with a number on it. That number corresponds to one of these categories. The guiding principle of this system is the smaller the number, the thinner the yarn.

NEEDLES/HOOKS

As you become more experienced as a knitter or crocheter, you will develop a preference for a certain type of needle or hook. Needles and hooks range from plastic and metal to bamboo and exotic woods like ebony—some are even gold plated! Beginner crocheters might want to consider buying hooks that have soft molded heads and avoid carved hooks with sharp-cut heads. Use whatever makes you most comfortable. Sometimes it is beneficial to knit back and forth on circular needles (instead of straight needles) because the cord connecting the needles can accommodate more stitches. Circular needles also make large, heavy projects a little easier to control and handle.

OTHER TOOLS

Scissors and a tape measure are a must. Often sizes are not imprinted on circular needles made from bamboo, wood, and metal, so a good needle gauge (with inches and centimeters) is recommended. It's handy to have a large-eyed, blunt needle for finishing and weaving in ends. You might find it useful to have stitch markers and cable needles for certain projects as well.

FINDING YOUR GAUGE

Determining your gauge may be a new concept if you haven't been knitting or crocheting for long. In general, gauge (sometimes called tension) is the number of stitches and rows measured over a number of inches (or centimeters) of your fabric. Every knitter or crocheter has her or his own particular tension, even when using the same needles and yarn as another person, so it is important to make sure you get the accurate gauge in order to make a wrap that will be the correct size indicated in the pattern.

Before you begin a project, you need to knit or crochet a swatch to find your gauge number, or "G" number. As a starting place, use the needle or hook size recommended by the manufacturer on the yarn label. Needles and hooks are sized in two ways: the actual size measured in millimeters (mm) and a descriptive size. Knitting needles have descriptive sizes that are expressed in numbers and crochet hooks have descriptive sizes that are expressed in letters. For example, 5 mm knitting needles are size 8 and 5 mm crochet hooks are size H-8.

Knit or crochet a swatch, using the stitch called for by your project, that is *at least* 4" (10 cm) wide. With a ruler, count the number of stitches in a 4" (10 cm) width (including half-stitches if there are any). Divide this number by 4 and you have your "G" number, or *the number of stitches per inch*. It is a good idea to take this measurement at a few different places on the fabric and average them. Your number may have half- or quarter-stitches represented as a decimal point if you did your division on a calculator.

If you did not get very close to the gauge in the pattern, go up a needle size if your gauge is too tight, or down a needle size if your gauge is too loose, and try again. Finding your gauge accurately is important for a proper fit. Many people knit and crochet for years before they ever do a gauge swatch. Once you start, you'll never do another project without one. Most swatches can be made in less than thirty minutes and it's worth taking the time.

There's no need to keep your gauge swatch as long as you save the right information. Photocopy the swatch and make sure you write the yarn details (brand name and standardized weight), needle or hook size, stitch pattern (e.g., stockinette or single crochet), number of stitches, number of rows, and the corresponding "G" number on the photocopy. It's good to start a file or a binder keeping your gauge information. That way you can avoid having to redo a gauge swatch for a new project made from a yarn you are already familiar with. Your gauge information can be saved by standardized weight or by yarn company. Familiarizing yourself with different gauges encourages you to experiment with sizing and developing your own designs.

SIZING

Most of the patterns for the wraps in this book are written in one size only. There's nothing to stop you from scaling the wrap down or up. All you need is a gauge swatch to work it out. If this is your first time adapting a pattern, start with a design from chapter 1 and work your way up to a more complicated pattern. For example, the Bowtie Wrap on page 78 has instructions for knitting a circular wrap that is knit in one piece and gathered in the front with a ribbon. The gauge is: 14 stitches + 20 rows = 4" (10 cm), and the "G" numbers are 3.5 stitches and 5 rows.

The original pattern is written for sizes 40", 45", and 50" and to be 17", 17", or 20" long. To make the same wrap in a smaller size, use the "G" number and adjust the pattern. For a wrap that is 32" (cm) around and 15" (cm) long, simply multiply the "G" number of stithces (3.5) by 32 (for the circumference) and the "G" number of rows (5) by 15 (for the length). Follow the instructions with the new number of stitches and rows. You can follow the same formula for other sizes and lengths.

To resize a wrap with shaping, choose a design from a later chapter such as Pleats Please in chapter 3.

The gauge is: 16 sts + 24 rows = 4" square and the "G" number is 4 stitches and 6 rows. This cashmere poncho is knit from the bottom to the top in four separate panels. It is fully fashioned with pleated decreases on both sides every 18 rows. In other words we decrease 12 stitches (6 stitches on each side) per panel on every pleat decrease row.

Let's turn this cropped poncho into a full-length poncho. We will change the length only and not the width. With this pattern, it makes sense to keep the pleats where they are and work the new length into the pattern without disturbing the design. To lengthen the poncho all we have to do is add one more pleat row, adding another 18 rows (3" [7.5 cm] in length) and 12 stitches (3" [7.5 cm] in width) per panel. Because we have added another pleat decrease row we need to add 12 sts to the cast-on instructions for each panel. Follow the pattern from Rows 1–19 with the extra 12 stitches and then start Row 20 as if it was Row 5 and complete the poncho as instructed.

KEEPING YOUR EDGES FLAT

Many of the wraps in this book are simple rectangular shapes. Unless the designs have ripple knit and crochet patterns like the flat wraps in chapter 2 you should consider some of the following edge techniques.

KNIT EDGES

These edges work particularly well for rectangular pieces done in stocking stitch:

Garter Stitch Edge: Knit every row. Garter stitch is very stretchy so use a needle at least 2 sizes smaller than you would for the rest of your wrap. When working in the round, you must knit 1 row, purl 1 row, as there is no wrong side.

1/1 Rib Edge: Ribs are alternating columns of knit and purl stitches. The simplest rib is 1x1 rib, which is knit 1, purl 1. Again, this is a very stretchy fabric and it is important to go down a needle size when using this stitch.

Over an even number of stitches:

Row 1: Knit 1, purl 1; repeat to end of row.

Repeat Row 1 for rib pattern.

2/2 Rib Edge: Ribs are alternating columns of knit and purl stitches. The simplest rib is 2/2 rib, which is knit 2, purl 2.

Over a multiple of 4 stitches:

Row 1: Knit 2, purl 2; repeat to end of row.

Repeat Row 1 for rib pattern.

Seed Stitch: A variation on a rib. Instead of knitting the knit stitches and purling the purl stitches, you alternate knit and purl stitches each row.

Over an odd number of stitches:

Row 1: *Knit 1, purl 1; repeat from * to last stitch, end knit 1.

Repeat Row 1 for pattern.

CROCHET EDGES

Simple Picot: In same stitch work [3 double crochet, chain 3, slip stitch in 3rd chain from hook, 3 double crochet].

Simple Picot Edging: Single crochet in one space, *[skip next space, picot in next space, skip next space, single crochet in next space], repeat from * around hat. Join round with a slip stitch in top of starting chain-3. Fasten off.

FUN FINISHES

Even the simplest wrap becomes a stunning success when you use a great finishing technique. Jazz up your wrap with embroidery or self trims like pom-poms, tassels, and rope cords.

STITCHES

These stitching techniques can be done with the same yarn you used for your project for a subtle effect; choose a contrasting yarn or thread for a bolder look.

Blanket Stitch: Sometimes called buttonhole stitch, blanket stitch is a great finishing touch on edges. Blanket stitch can also be used as embellishment or to finish wrap edges.

Step 1. Using a blunt, large-eyed yarn needle, secure the yarn by gently attaching it to a stitch on the wrong side of work. Leave a 3" (8 cm) tail to weave in later.

Step 2. Draw the needle through to the right side of work, close to the edge.

Step 3. Bring the needle above the yarn and insert it a couple of stitches to the right of where you first inserted it (see below).

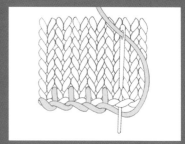

Blanket stitch.

1-1. Invisible seam—stockinette stitch.

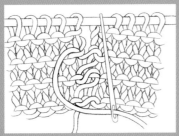

1-2. Invisible seam—garter stitch.

Step 4. Pull the needle past the edge of the wrap to complete the stitch.

Repeat Steps 3 and 4, inserting the needle the same number of stitches apart for even spacing.

Invisible Seaming: Invisible seaming is a sturdy, almost invisible stitch used to sew two panels together. It can be sewn (vertically) on the side seam or (horizontally) on two bound-off edges. Invisible seaming is worked on the right side, with a long yarn end and a large-eyed, blunt sewing needle. Start at the upper or lower edge by joining the two edges. Begin invisible seaming by catching two horizontal bars just inside the edge of the first stitch and carry the thread across to the other side, stitching under the next pair of bars inside the edge of the first stitch (see illustration 1–1). Pull the sewing thread every couple of stitches but do not gather. There should be some ease. The seam will join together and be nearly invisible. The same technique can be used to join two bound-off edges (see illustration 1–2).

On ribbed designs, remember that one stitch is taken up with the seam allowance. For instance, panels with a 2/2 rib should start and finish with two knit stitches at the beginning and end of all sides to be joined. You will loose one plain stitch at the edge of both panels to be joined, but you are still left with two plain when you join the panels with mattress stitch so you don't break the 2/2 pattern of the rib. See how the 2/2 rib on Pleats Please in chapter 3 comes together without breaking up the 2/2 rib at the hem.

SELF TRIMS

Pom-Poms: You can make pom-poms big or little, multicolored or solid. Purchase a pom-pom maker, or use cardboard and follow the instructions. To make, cut a piece of cardboard the size of the finished pom-pom and wrap the yarn tightly around the cardboard until cardboard is completely covered (see illustration 2–1). Slide the yarn

2-1. Wrap yarn around cardboard.

2-2. Cut strands at both ends.

2-3. Trim pom-pom.

off the cardboard and tie tightly around the middle. Cut loops at both ends (see illustration 2–2). Trim pom-pom if necessary (see illustration 2–3).

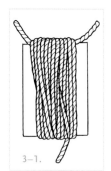

3–1.

3–2.

3–3.

Rope Cords: Cut 6 strands of yarn for the tie, each approximately 94" (239 cm) long. If you are using a bulky yarn for the tie, you may want to use fewer than 6 strands of yarn to make the cord. Hold lengths together and tie a knot at each end. Anchor one end and twist the other end clockwise many times until the piece is very tight and almost kinked. Hold rope in the center and release both ends, allowing them to wrap around each other.

Tassels: Tassels add a dramatic finish to just about any wrap. To make a tassel, cut a piece of cardboard the length you want the finished tassel to be. Wrap yarn around cardboard, remembering that more yarn means a fuller, heavier tassel (see illustration 3–1). Slip a piece of yarn under one end and tie in a knot (see illustration 3–2). Cut the other end open. With a separate piece of yarn, wrap and tie tassel near top (see illustration 3–3).

Crochet Corkscrews: Make a chain the desired length. Double crochet in 3rd chain from hook, 2 more double crochets in same chain, 3 double crochets in each chain to end. Pull end through last double crochet to secure. Cut yarn, leaving tail for sewing. The Bookworm Boa in chapter 1 is made from corkscrews.

EMBELLISHMENTS

The possibilities for embellishments are endless. Purchased brooches or pins make easy embellishments that double as clever closures. Many of the wraps in this book can be worn and closed in several ways so it makes sense to have a closure that can also be adaptable. Websites like mjtrim.com sell all kinds of pins and closures ranging from Deco pins to tab snap closures. Also, keep your eyes peeled for funky vintage brooches and pins at your local flea market. We have included instructions for basic embroidered stitches as well as knit and crochet instructions for flowers that will dress up any wrap—glue a pinback on a flower for an instant corsage!

EMBROIDERY STITCHES

Running Stitch: This basic sewing stitch looks fresh and new when done with yarn on knitted or crocheted fabric. Use a blunt, large-eyed needle and insert it into the

Running stitch.

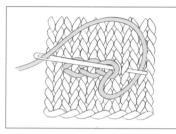

Chain stitch.

eyed needle and insert it into the fabric from the wrong side to the right side, leaving a 3" (8 cm) tail of yarn to weave in later. Insert the needle back to the wrong side; be careful not to pull the yarn too tightly or it will distort the fabric. Continue for desired length.

Chain Stitch: Chain stitch is a simple embroidery technique that looks great on knitted and crocheted fabric because it mimics the shape of stitches. Once mastered, it is easy to "draw" with this method either following a chart or working freeform. Personalize a simple wrap by embroidering the recipient's initials or an heirloom piece with your own initials. Choose a yarn smooth enough to glide through the finished fabric.

Step 1. Using a blunt, large-eyed yarn needle secure the yarn by gently attaching it to a stitch on the wrong side of work. Leave a 3" (8 cm) tail for weaving in.

Step 2. Draw the needle through to the right side of work.

Step 3. Create a small loop by inserting the needle back where it came out. Secure the loop with your finger. Pull the needle through, above the loop, creating a chain stitch (see Chain stitch illustration). Do not pull too tightly or fabric will warp.

Repeat step 3 in any direction as desired, being careful to space stitches evenly.

FLOWERS

Crochet Flowers

Chain 4. Join with slip stitch to form a ring.

Round 1 Chain 1 (counts as 1 single crochet), work 11 single crochet into ring. Join round with slip stitch in chain-1.

Round 2 [Chain 3, skip next stitch, single crochet in next stitch] 6 times—6 chain-3 loops.

Round 3 [In next chain-3 loop work (single crochet, half double crochet, 3 double crochet, half double crochet, single crochet)] 6 times. Join round with a slip stitch in first single crochet. Fasten off.

Knit Flowers

Cast on 42 stitches.

Row 1 (wrong side) Purl.

Row 2 Knit 2, *knit 1, slip this stitch back to left needle, lift next 5 stitches on left needle over this stitch and off needle, yarn over twice, knit the first stitch again, knit 2; repeat from *—27 stitches.

Row 3 Purl 1, *purl 2 together, drop 1 of the yarn over loops, (knit into the front and back) twice in remaining yarn over of previous row, purl 1; repeat from * to last stitch, purl 1—32 stitches.

Row 4 Knit 1, *knit 3 together; repeat from *, end knit 1—12 stitches.

Row 5 *Purl 2 together; repeat from *—6 stitches; slip second, third, fourth, fifth, and sixth stitches over first stitch. Fasten off and sew seam.

1.

EASY DOES IT

The five wraps in this chapter are perfect for beginners who have learned the nuts and bolts of knitting and crocheting. These patterns run the gamut of shapes and introduce projects that include a round cape, a three-dimensional boa, a flat blanket poncho, and a tubular shrug. They may look complex, but they are all rewarding beginner projects that utilize basic knit and purl stitches or single and double crochet.

BOOKWORM BOA

DESIGNED BY CATHY MAGUIRE

CROCHET/BEGINNER

Easy crocheted corkscrews are twisted together for a colorful, glamorous accessory.

SIZE
60" (152.5 cm) long, approximately

MATERIALS

LION BRAND LION BOUCLÉ
79% ACRYLIC, 20% MOHAIR,
1% NYLON
2½ OZ (70 G) 57 YD (97 M) BALL

6 balls each #210 Wild Berries,
#211 Tutti Frutti, or colors of your
choice

• Size J-10 (6 mm) crochet hook *or
size to obtain gauge*

GAUGE
11 double crochet + 6 rows = 4"
(10 cm).
Be sure to check your gauge.

BOA (MAKE 2, 1 IN EACH COLOR)

Row 1 Chain 15, 2 double crochet in 4th chain from hook, 3 double crochet in each of next 9 chains, slip stitch in same stitch as last double crochet.

Repeat Row 1 for 49 more times, or work until Boa measures 60" (152.5 cm) or desired length from beginning, joining more yarn as necessary. Fasten off. Weave in ends.

FINISHING
Twist Boas together to wear.

WRAPTURE

DESIGNED BY VLADIMIR TERIOKHIN

CROCHET/EASY

This chic crocheted wrap can be worn with the opening to the front or the side. Made with bulky yarn and a large hook, you'll be wearing it in no time!

SIZE

One size fits most
Width 40" (101.5 cm)
Length 16" (40.5 cm) (including neckband)

MATERIALS

LION BRAND HOMESPUN
98% ACRYLIC, 2% POLYESTER
6 OZ (170 G) 185 YD (167 M) SKEIN

3 skeins #312 Edwardian (main color) or color of your choice

LION BRAND FUN FUR
100% POLYESTER
1¾ OZ (50 G) 64 YD (58.5 M) BALL

3 balls each #195 Hot Pink (contrasting color 1), #153 Black (contrasting color 2), or colors of your choice

• Size K-10.5 (6.5 mm) crochet hook *or size to obtain gauge*

• Stitch markers

GAUGE

12.75 stitches + 8 rows = 4" (10 cm) over double crochet using main color.
Be sure to check your gauge.

NOTES

Work with 1 strand each of contrasting color 1 and contrasting color 2 held together for collar. It's sometimes difficult to see the stitches when working with furry yarn. For best results, count stitches as you work each row to make sure you do not skip or miss a stitch.

TIES/NECKBAND

With main color, chain 7.
Row 1 Double crochet in 4th chain from hook and in each chain across—5 stitches. Chain 3. Turn.
Row 2 Double crochet in each stitch across. Chain 3. Turn. Repeat Row 2 for pattern stitch and work even until piece measures 16" (40.5 cm) from beginning.
Mark each side of last row for beginning of Neckband. Continue to work even until Neckband measures 40" (101.5 cm) above marked row.
Mark each side of last row for end of Neckband. Continue to work even for 16" (40.5 cm); piece should measure 72" (183 cm) from beginning. Fasten off.

BODY

Join main color with a slip stitch at a Neckband marker.
Row 1 Chain 3, work 128 double crochet evenly spaced along neckband to next marker. Chain 3. Turn. Continue in double crochet and work even until body measures 14½" (37 cm) from beginning (not including Neckband). Fasten off.

COLLAR

With 1 strand each of contrasting color 1 and contrasting color 2 held together, join yarns with a slip stitch at a Neckband marker opposite body.

Row 1 Chain 1, work 138 single crochet evenly spaced along Neckband to next marker. Chain 1. Turn. Continue in single crochet until collar measures 8" (20.5 cm) from beginning (not including Neckband). Fasten off.

10 (10 ¼)"

5 ½ (6 ½)"

3"

64 (68)"

3"

VINTAGE SHRUG

VINTAGE SHRUG

DESIGNED BY VLADIMIR TERIOKHIN

KNIT/EASY

Even if you are a beginning knitter you can make this one-piece shrug, knit in rib and garter stitch from wrist to wrist.

SIZE

S/M (M/L)

Cuff-to-Cuff 70 (74)" (178 [188] cm)

Length 18 (18¾)" (45.5 [47.5] cm) as worn

Note Pattern is written for smaller size with changes for larger size in parentheses. When only one number is given, it applies to both sizes. To follow pattern more easily, circle all numbers pertaining to your size before beginning.

MATERIALS

 LION BRAND WOOL-EASE 80% ACRYLIC, 20% WOOL 3 OZ (85 G) 197 YD (180 M) BALL

5 balls #107 Blue Heather or color of your choice

• Size 6 (4 mm) 24" (60 cm) circular needle *or size to obtain gauge*

• Large-eyed, blunt needle

GAUGE

28 stitches + 32 rows = 4" (10 cm) in garter stitch (knit every row). *Be sure to check your gauge.*

NOTE

Shrug is worked in one piece from one cuff across to the other cuff.

SHRUG

Starting at left cuff, cast on 40 (46) stitches. Do not join. Work back and forth in knit 1, purl 1 rib for 3" (7.5 cm). Change to garter stitch and increase 1 stitch each end every other row 15 times—70 (76) stitches. Work even until piece measures 63 (67)" (160 [170] cm) from cast-on edge. Decrease 1 stitch each end every other row 15 times—40 (46) stitches. Work in knit 1, purl 1 rib for 3" (7.5 cm). Bind off loosely.

FINISHING

Fold piece in half along long edge so that ribbing is at left and right ends. Sew each cuff and arm seam for 17" (43 cm), leaving 36 (40)" (91.5 [101.5] cm) open in middle. Pick up and knit 194 (202) stitches around opening. Join and work in rounds of knit 1, purl 1 rib for 4" (10 cm). Bind off loosely.

BLANKET PONCHO

DESIGNED BY LORNA MISER

KNIT/EASY

Combine a richly hued bouclé yarn with a variegated ribbon yarn for a striped poncho with panache.

SIZE

Width 33" (84 cm)
Length 22" (56 cm)

MATERIALS

 LION BRAND COLOR WAVES 83% ACRYLIC, 17% POLYESTER 3 OZ (85 G) 125 YD (425 M) SKEIN

4 skeins #313 Sunset Red (main color) or color of your choice

 LION BRAND INCREDIBLE 100% POLYMIDE 1¾ OZ (50 G) 110 YD (100 M) SKEIN

2 balls #208 Copper Penny (contrasting color) or color of your choice

- Size 10 (6 mm) knitting needles *or size to obtain gauge*

- Large-eyed, blunt needle

GAUGE

10 stitches + 17 rows = 4" (10 cm) in pattern stitch.
Be sure to check your gauge.

PATTERN STITCH (EVEN NUMBER OF STITCHES)

Rows 1–6 With main color, knit.
Row 7 (Right Side) With contrasting color, leaving a 12" (30.5 cm) tail, knit.
Row 8 With contrasting color, purl 1, [yarn over, purl 2 together] to last stitch, purl 1. Cut contrasting color, leaving a 12" (30.5 cm) tail.
Repeat Rows 1–8 for pattern stitch.

NOTE

Count stitches after knitting Row 7 of each repeat. It is the easiest row on which to see the stitches clearly and check that there are the correct number before working the eyelet row. When starting Row 7, leave a 12" (30.5 cm) tail of contrasting color; then cut a tail 12" (30.5 cm) long after working Row 8. Tie the 2 ends together in a knot close to edge. One edge of each piece is fringed as it is knit; the opposite edge of each piece is sewn to form the top of the arm and shoulders with neck opening at center.

WRAP (MAKE 2)

With main color, cast on 54 stitches. Work Rows 1–8 of pattern stitch 17 times; then work Rows 1–6 once more. Bind off loosely.

FINISHING

With wrong sides together, sew shoulder seams invisibly, leaving center 11" (28 cm) open for neck. Cut 26" (66 cm) lengths of contrasting color and knot these over existing fringe for more fullness. Trim fringe if necessary.

THE VELVET PRINCESS

DESIGNED BY
PATRICIA WENIGER

CROCHET/EASY

Your favorite little girl will feel like royalty when she wears this buttery-soft wrap. The sweet-as-pie cape is crocheted with a large hook and works up in a flash.

SIZE

Circumference 19" (48.5 cm) at neck; 56" (142 cm) at lower edge
Length 13" (33 cm)

MATERIALS

 LION BRAND VELVETSPUN
100% POLYESTER
3 OZ (85 G) 54 YD (49 M) BALL

4 balls #144 Lavender or color of your choice

- Size K-10.5 (6.5 mm) crochet hook *or size to obtain gauge*

- 1 yard (1 m) of 1½" (38 mm) wide organza ribbon to match

- One large hook-and-eye set

- Sewing needle and thread to match yarn

GAUGE

8 stitches + 6 rows = 4" (10 cm) in pattern.
Be sure to check your gauge.

CAPELET

Starting at neck edge, chain 38.

Row 1 (Right Side) Single crochet in 2nd chain from hook and in each chain across. Turn—37 single crochet.

Row 2 Chain 3, *double crochet in next single crochet, 2 double crochet in next single crochet; repeat from * across. Turn—55 stitches.

Row 3 Chain 1, single crochet in each double crochet across. Turn.

Row 4 Chain 3, skip first single crochet, double crochet in each single crochet across. Turn—55 stitches.

Row 5 Repeat Row 3.

Row 6 Chain 3, *double crochet in next 2 single crochet, 2 double crochet in next single crochet; repeat from * across. Turn—73 stitches.

Rows 7–8 Repeat Rows 3–4.

Row 9 Repeat Row 3.

Row 10 Chain 3, *double crochet in next 3 single crochet, 2 double crochet in next single crochet; repeat from * across. Turn—91 stitches.

Rows 11–12 Repeat Rows 3–4.

Row 13 Repeat Row 3.

Row 14 Chain 3, double crochet in same single crochet, *double crochet in next 4 single crochet, 2 double crochet in next single crochet; repeat from * across. Turn—110 stitches.

Rows 15–16 Repeat Rows 3–4.

Row 17 Repeat Row 3. Do not fasten off.

EDGING

Working across side edge of Capelet, chain 1, single crochet evenly spaced across to next corner, 2 single crochet in corner stitch; working across opposite side of foundation chain, *chain 1, skip next chain, single crochet in next chain; repeat from * across to next corner, 2 single crochet in next corner stitch; single crochet evenly spaced across side edge to next corner. Fasten off.

FINISHING

With sewing needle and thread, sew hook and eye to corners on top edge of Capelet. Weave ribbon through the spaces of Edging and tie in a bow at center front.

2.
RIPPLE WRAPS

This chapter teaches you about knit and crochet techniques with stitch patterns in which a certain number of stitches and rows are required to form one complete pattern. The ripple patterns are formed by completing all increases at one point in the pattern and all decreases at another. This chapter includes a classic crocheted ripple wrap and two knit ripple wraps, one with lacy increases and one with increases that produce a solid fabric. None of the pieces are shaped, so you can concentrate on patterning and mixing colors while becoming familiar with pattern stitches.

MAGIC CHEVRONS

DESIGNED BY KATHERINE ENG

CROCHET/INTERMEDIATE

It's hard to believe that just one yarn is used for this multicolored crocheted wrap—the yarn is dyed with extra-long color repeats to create its own stripes. There is minimal finishing and you never have to change colors.

SIZE

22" wide x 68" long (56 x 172.5 cm)

MATERIALS

 LION BRAND HOMESPUN
98% ACRYLIC, 2% POLYESTER
6 OZ (170 G) 185 YD (167 M)
SKEIN

4 skeins #377 Harvest or color of your choice

- Size N-13 (9 mm) crochet hook
  or size to obtain gauge

GAUGE

8 stitches = 4" (10 cm); Rows 1–3 = 2½" (6.5 cm).
Be sure to check your gauge.

STITCH EXPLANATIONS

Single crochet 2 together (single crochet decrease) Insert hook into stitch and draw up a loop. Insert hook into next stitch and draw up a loop. Yarn over, draw through all 3 loops on hook.

Shell [3 double crochet, chain 2, 3 double crochet] in same stitch.

NOTE

Wrap is made of 2 halves worked off a center foundation chain.

FIRST HALF

Chain 42.

Row 1 (Wrong Side) Single crochet in 2nd chain from hook and in each chain across. Turn—41 single crochet.

Row 2 Chain 1, single crochet in first single crochet, *chain 1, skip next single crochet, half double crochet in next single crochet, chain 1, skip next single crochet, [double crochet, chain 2, double crochet] in next single crochet, chain 1, skip next single crochet, half double crochet in next single crochet, chain 1, skip next single crochet, single crochet in next single crochet; repeat from * across. Turn—5 chain 2-spaces.

Row 3 Chain 1, single crochet 2 together in first 2 stitches, chain 1, single crochet in next chain 1-space, chain 1, [single crochet, chain 2, single crochet] in next chain 2-space, *[chain 1, single crochet] in each of next 2 chain 1-spaces, [single crochet, chain 1] in each of next 2 chain 1-spaces, [single crochet, chain 2, single crochet] in next chain 2-space; repeat from * across to last 5 stitches, chain 1, single crochet in next chain 1-space, chain 1, single crochet 2 together in last 2 stitches. Turn—5 chain 2-spaces.

Row 4 Chain 1, single crochet 2 together in first 2 stitches, chain 1,

half double crochet in next chain 1-space, chain 1, [double crochet, chain 2, double crochet] in next chain 2-space, *chain 1, half double crochet in next chain 1-space, chain 1, single crochet in each of next 2 chain 1-spaces, chain 1, half double crochet in next chain 1-space, chain 1, [double crochet, chain 2, double crochet] in next chain 2-space; repeat from * across to last 5 stitches, chain 1, half double crochet in next chain 1-space, chain 1, single crochet 2 together in last 2 stitches. Turn—5 chain 2-spaces.

Rows 5–56 Repeat Rows 3–4. Fasten off.

SECOND HALF

Row 1 With wrong side facing, working across opposite side of foundation chain, join yarn in first chain. Chain 1, single crochet in each chain across. Turn—41 single crochet.

Rows 2–56 Repeat Rows 2–56 of First Half. Do not fasten off.

BORDER

Round 1 (Right Side) Working across long edge of wrap, chain 1, *work 1 single crochet in each of next 56 row-end stitches, single crochet in foundation chain, single crochet in each of next 56 row-end stitches to next corner, chain 2, work in established pattern of Row 3 of First Half across short edge of wrap, chain 2; repeat from * around. Join with slip stitch in first single crochet.

Round 2 Chain 1, **single crochet in first single crochet, *chain 1, skip next 2 single crochet, shell in next single crochet, chain 1, skip next 2 single crochet, single crochet in next single crochet *; repeat from * to * 9 more times, chain 1, skip next single crochet, shell in next single crochet, chain 1 skip next single crochet, single crochet in next single crochet; repeat from * to * 9 times, [single crochet, chain 2, single crochet] in corner chain 2-space, work in established pattern of Row 4 of First Half across short edge of wrap, [single crochet, chain 2, single crochet] in corner chain 2-space; repeat from ** around; join with slip stitch in first single crochet.

Round 3 Slip stitch in first chain 1-space, chain 1, **[single crochet in chain 1-space, chain 1, skip next double crochet, single crochet in next double crochet, chain 1, (single crochet, chain 2, single crochet) in next chain 2-space, chain 1, skip next double crochet, single crochet in next double crochet, chain 1, single crochet in next chain 1-space, chain 2] across to next corner chain 2-space, [single crochet, chain 2, single crochet] in each chain 1-space and each chain 2-space across short edge of wrap, ending in corner chain 2-space, chain 2; repeat from ** around. Join with slip stitch in first single crochet.

FINISHING

Fasten off. Weave in ends.

ROCK AND RIPPLE

DESIGNED BY STEPHANIE KLOSE

KNIT/EASY

Knit a funky multicolored showstopper fit for a megastar. This wrap shows how effectively differently textured yarns work together.

SIZE
20" x 70" (51 x 178 cm)

MATERIALS

 LION BRAND LION BOUCLÉ 79% ACRYLIC, 20% MOHAIR, 1% NYLON
2½ OZ (70 G) 57 YD (97 M) BALL

6 balls #205 Sorbet (A) or color of your choice

 LION BRAND FUN FUR 100% POLYESTER
1¾ OZ (50 G) 65 YD (58 M) BALL

1 ball each #132 Olive (B), #194 Lime (C), #112 Raspberry (D), #133 Tangerine (E), or colors of your choice

• Size 15 (10 mm) knitting needles *or size to obtain gauge*

GAUGE
11 stitches + 10 rows = 4" (10 cm) in Feather & Fan pattern with A.
Be sure to check your gauge.

PATTERN STITCH

FEATHER & FAN (MULTIPLE OF 18 STITCHES + 2)

Rows 1–2 Knit.
Row 3 Knit 1, *[knit 2 together] 3 times, [yarn over, knit 1] 6 times, [knit 2 together] 3 times; repeat from * to last stitch, knit 1.
Row 4 Purl.
Repeat Rows 1–4 for Feather & Fan pattern.

SHAWL
With A, cast on 56 stitches.
*With A, work Feather & Fan Rows 1–4 twice. Break yarn.
With 1 strand each of B and C held together, repeat Rows 1–4 once.
Break yarns.
With A, repeat Rows 1–4 twice.
Break yarn.
With 1 strand each of D and E held together, repeat Rows 1–4 once.

Break yarns.
Repeat from * 7 times or to desired length, ending with 2 repeats of Rows 1–4 with A.

FINISHING
Bind off loosely. Weave in ends.

NEW WAVE

DESIGNED BY STEPHANIE KLOSE

KNIT/EASY

Combine rich colors and textures for a sophisticated wrap you'll throw on over everything.

SIZE
27½" wide x 65" long
(70 x 165 cm)

MATERIALS

LION BRAND LANDSCAPES 50% WOOL, 50% ACRYLIC 1¾ OZ (50 G) 55 YD (50 M) BALL

10 balls #275 Autumn Trails (A) or color of your choice

LION BRAND CHENILLE THICK & QUICK 91% ACRYLIC, 9% RAYON 100 YD (91 M) SKEIN

1 skein each #125 Chocolate (B), #110 Marine (C), #143 Bordeaux (D), or colors of your choice

• Size 13 (9 mm) knitting needles or size to obtain gauge

GAUGE
8 stitches + 10 rows = 4" (10 cm) in pattern stitch with A or B. *Be sure to check your gauge.*

STITCH EXPLANATION
Ssk (slip, slip, knit) Slip next 2 stitches as if to knit, one at a time, to right needle. Insert left needle into fronts of these 2 stitches and knit them together.

PATTERN STITCH (MULTIPLE OF 11 STITCHES)
Rows 1–6 Knit.
Rows 7, 9, 11, and 13 *Knit 2 together, knit 2, [knit into front and back of next stitch] 2 times, knit 3, ssk; repeat from * to end of row.
Rows 8, 10, 12, and 14 Purl.
Repeat Rows 1–14 for pattern stitch.

STRIPE SEQUENCE
*6 rows B, 8 rows A, 6 rows C, 8 rows A, 6 rows D, 8 rows A; repeat from *.

WRAP
With B, cast on 55 stitches. Work in pattern stitch following Stripe Sequence until piece measures approximately 65" (165 cm), ending with 6 rows D.

FINISHING
Bind off all stitches. Weave in ends.

3.
CABLE-KNIT WRAPS

Cable knitting can appear complicated, but it is a simple method of using a cable needle to cross one set of stitches over another. This chapter introduces you to simple rope cables, bobbles, pleats, and cable and lace patterns. A word on cable knitting: It is important to remember that cables, like ribs, compress your knitting widthwise compared to a flat knitted fabric. Allowances are made for this in all our pattern instructions. Dickie Do includes instructions for a simple cable that starts halfway into the pattern and gets knitted to the neck and shoulders. The Rope Wrap will teach you the bobble, another staple of textured knitting.

DICKIE DO

DESIGNED BY CATHY MAGUIRE

KNIT/EASY

This dickie is a great introduction to the world of cables. Several simple rope cables are knit in thick yarn, making this a fast and fun project that he'll wear all winter.

SIZE

17" wide x 14½" long (43 x 37 cm) without turtleneck

MATERIALS

 LION BRAND WOOL-EASE THICK & QUICK (6) 80% ACRYLIC, 20% WOOL 6 OZS (170 G) 108 YD (98 M) BALL

2 balls #149 Charcoal or color of your choice

- Size 13 (9 mm) knitting needles *or size to obtain gauge*

- Size 13 (9 mm) 16" (40.5 cm) circular needle

- Cable needle

- Stitch holders (6)

- Large-eyed, blunt needle

GAUGE

9 stitches + 12 rows = 4" (10 cm) in stockinette stitch (knit on right side, purl on wrong side).
Be sure to check your gauge.

STITCH EXPLANATIONS

C4F (cable 4 front) Slip 2 stitches to cable needle and hold to front of work, knit next 2 stitches, knit 2 stitches from cable needle.

Grafting Holding the 2 needles parallel with wrong sides of fabric together, thread a large-eyed, blunt needle with one of the yarn ends and work as follows:
Insert needle as if to purl into first stitch on Front Piece. Insert needle as if to knit into first stitch on Back. Then follow steps 1–4 as outlined below.

Step 1 Insert needle as if to knit through first stitch on front needle and let the stitch drop from needle.

Step 2 Insert needle into 2nd stitch on front needle as if to purl and pull the yarn through, leaving stitch on the needle.

Step 3 Insert needle into first stitch on back needle as if to purl and let it drop from the needle, then

Step 4 Insert needle as if to knit through 2nd stitch on back needle and pull the yarn through, leaving stitch on needle. Repeat steps 1–4 until all stitches are gone. When finished, adjust tension as necessary. Weave in ends.

FRONT

Cast on 38 stitches.

Row 1 (Right Side) *Knit 2, purl 2; repeat from *, ending knit 2.

Row 2 *Purl 2, knit 2; repeat from *, ending purl 2.

Rows 3–4 Repeat Rows 1–2.

Row 5 Knit 2, purl 2, knit 30, purl 2, knit 2.

Row 6 Purl 2, knit 2, purl 30, knit 2, purl 2.

Rows 7–16 Repeat Rows 5–6.

Row 17 (Cable Row) Knit 2, purl 2, [knit 3, purl 1, cable 4 front, purl 1] 3 times, knit 3, purl 2, knit 2.

Row 18 Purl 2, knit 2, [purl 3, knit 1, purl 4, knit 1] 3 times, purl 3, knit 2, purl 2.

Row 19 Knit 2, purl 2, [knit 3, purl 1, knit 4, purl 1] 3 times, knit 3, purl 2, knit 2.

Row 20 Repeat Row 18.

Rows 21–24 Repeat Rows 17–20.

Rows 25–26 Repeat Rows 17–18.

Row 27 Knit 2, purl 2, knit 3, purl 1, knit 2, slip 10 stitches just worked onto holder for shoulder, knit 2, purl 1, knit 3, purl 1, knit 4, purl 1, knit 3, purl 1, knit 2, slip 18 stitches just worked onto a 2nd holder for neck, knit 2, purl 1, knit 3, purl 2, knit 2, slip 10 stitches just worked onto a 3rd holder for shoulder.

BACK

Work as for Front through Row 24.

Rows 25–28 Repeat Rows 17–20.

Rows 29–30 Repeat Rows 17–18.

Row 31 Repeat Row 27.

NECK

With right side facing and circular needle, join yarn at beginning of Front Neck stitches and work across in knit 2, purl 2 rib. Continue in rib across Back Neck stitches. Join for working in the round—36 stitches. Work in knit 2, purl 2 rib for 14 rounds. Bind off.

FINISHING

Graft shoulder seams. Weave in ends.

ROPE WRAP

DESIGNED BY MARY ANNENBERG

KNIT/INTERMEDIATE

Practice cables with this cozy wrap. The bobbles in the center panel add extra texture.

SIZE
11" x 52" (28 x 132 cm)

MATERIALS

 LION BRAND JIFFY THICK & QUICK 100% ACRYLIC 5 OZ (140 G) 84 YD (76 M) BALL

5 balls #212 Adirondacks or color of your choice

• Size 15 (10 mm) knitting needles *or size to obtain gauge*

• Size P-15 (10 mm) crochet hook

• Cable needle

GAUGE
8 stitches + 13 rows = 4" (10 cm) in Panel 1 pattern.
Be sure to check your gauge.

STITCH EXPLANATIONS
RT (right twist) Knit 2 together and leave stitches on left needle; with right needle, go between the 2 stitches and knit the first stitch again. Drop both stitches from left needle.

2/2LC (2 over 2 left cross) Slip 2 stitches to cable needle and hold in front, knit 2, then knit 2 from cable needle.

2/2RC (2 over 2 right cross) Slip 2 stitches to cable needle and hold in back, knit 2, then knit 2 from cable needle.

2/3RC (2 over 3 right cross) Slip 3 stitches to cable needle and hold in back, knit 2, then knit 3 from cable needle.

3/3LC (3 over 3 left cross) Slip 3 stitches to cable needle and hold in front, knit 3, then knit 3 from cable needle.

3/3RC (3 over 3 right cross) Slip 3 stitches to cable needle and hold in back, knit 3, then knit 3 from cable needle.

MB (make bobble) [knit 1, purl 1, knit 1, purl 1, knit 1] in same stitch, pass 2nd stitch on right needle over first, 3rd stitch over first, 4th stitch over first, 5th stitch over first to make small bobble.

NOTE
Shawl is made of 5 panels that are crocheted together. Begin each panel with a new ball of yarn; remaining yarn is used for finishing.

PANEL 1
Cast on 24 stitches.

Rows 1, 3, and 5 (Wrong Side) Knit 1, purl 7, knit 1, purl 6, knit 1, purl 7, knit 1.

Rows 2 and 4 (Right Side) Purl 1, RT, knit 3, RT, purl 1, knit 6, purl 1, RT, knit 3, RT, purl 1.

Row 6 purl 1, RT, knit 3, RT, purl 1, LC, purl 1, RT, knit 3, RT, purl 1.

Rows 7, 9, 11, and 13 Repeat Row 1.

Rows 8, 10, and 12 Repeat Row 2.

Rows 14–29 Repeat Rows 6–13.

Row 30 Repeat Row 6.
Rows 31 and 33 Repeat Row 1.
Row 32 Repeat Row 2.
Bind off, leaving a 54" (137 cm) tail for joining.

PANEL 2
Cast on 16 stitches.
Rows 1, 3, and 5 (Wrong Side) Knit 1, purl 4, knit 1, purl 4, knit 1, purl 4, knit 1.
Rows 2 and 4 (Right Side) Purl 1, knit 4, purl 1, knit 4, purl 1, knit 4, purl 1.
Row 6 Purl 1, LC, purl 1, LC, purl 1, LC, purl 1.
Rows 7–30 Repeat Rows 1–6.
Rows 31 and 33 Repeat Row 1.
Row 32 Repeat Row 2.
Bind off, leaving a 54" (137 cm) tail for joining.

PANEL 3 (CENTER)
Cast on 21 stitches.
Rows 1, 3, and 5 (Wrong Side) Knit 1, purl 2, knit 2, purl 2, knit 1, purl 5, knit 1, purl 2, knit 2, purl 2, knit 1.

Rows 2 and 4 (Right Side) Purl 1, knit 6, purl 1, knit 5, purl 1, knit 6, purl 1.
Row 6 Purl 1, knit 6, purl 1, RC, purl 1, knit 6, purl 1.
Rows 7 and 9 Repeat Row 1.
Row 8 Repeat Row 2.
Row 10 Purl 1, knit 6, purl 1, knit 2, MB, knit 2, purl 1, knit 6, purl 1.
Rows 11 and 13 Repeat Row 1.
Row 12 Repeat Row 2.
Rows 14–29 Repeat Rows 6–13.
Row 30 Repeat Row 6.
Rows 31 and 33 Repeat Row 1.
Row 32 Repeat Row 2.
Bind off, leaving a 54" (137 cm) tail for joining.

PANEL 4
Repeat Panel 2, working RC in place of LC.

PANEL 5
Repeat Panel 1, working RC in place of LC.

FINISHING
With bound-off edges at top, crochet panels together using a slip stitch. Join fullest remaining ball to left bottom corner of piece. With right side facing, work 2 rounds single crochet evenly spaced around outside edge.
Next row Chain 1, single crochet in first single crochet, *chain 2, skip 1 single crochet, single crochet in next single crochet; repeat from * across bottom edge. Fasten off.

FRINGE
Cut remaining yarn into 10" (25.5 cm) lengths. Using 3 strands per Fringe, fold in half to form a loop. Insert crochet hook into one of the crocheted spaces along bottom edge of shawl and draw loop through. Draw ends of Fringe through loop and tighten. Repeat for each crocheted space along bottom edge of shawl.

CABLE AND LACE PONCHO

DESIGNED BY VLADIMIR TERIOKHIN

KNIT/INTERMEDIATE

Combine your cable- and lace-knitting skills when making this poncho with a gorgeous allover textured pattern.

SIZE

Women's S (M/L)

Circumference 17 1/2 (18)" (44.5 [45.5] cm) at neck; 52 3/4 (57 1/2)" (134 [146] cm) at lower edge

Length 16 1/2 (18)" (42 [45.5] cm)

Note Pattern is written for smaller size with changes for larger size in parentheses. When only one number is given, it applies to both sizes. To follow pattern more easily, circle all numbers pertaining to your size before beginning.

MATERIALS

 LION BRAND WOOL-EASE CHUNKY
80% ACRYLIC, 20% WOOL
5 OZ (140 G) 153 YD (140 M) BALL

3 (4) balls #173 Willow or color of your choice

- Size 10 (6 mm) 32" (81 cm) and 16" (40.5 cm) circular needles *or size to obtain gauge*

- Stitch markers

GAUGE

15 stitches + 19 rows = 4" (10 cm) in pattern stitch.
Be sure to check your gauge.

NOTE

Poncho is worked in one piece in the round from bottom to top. It is helpful to use one color of marker to indicate beginning of round, and 3 markers of a different color to mark decrease points. Work chart from right to left on every round.

PONCHO

With longer circular needle, cast on 176 (192) stitches loosely. Place marker and join for working in the round, being careful not to twist. Work in purl 1, knit 1 rib for 1 1/2" (3.8 cm).

Increase round *[Purl 1, knit 1] 3 times, knit and purl into next stitch, knit 1; repeat from * 21 (23) more times—198 (216) stitches.

Next round Work Round 1 of chart,

repeating pattern for entire round. Work even in charted pattern until piece measures 3" (7.5 cm) from beginning.

Next round Continuing in pattern, work 86 (95) stitches, place marker, work 13 stitches, place marker, work 86 (95) stitches, place marker, work 13 stitches to beginning marker.

Next round Slip first marker, *purl 2 together, work in pattern to 2 stitches before next marker, purl 2 together, slip marker, work next 13 stitches in pattern, slip marker; repeat from * once more—194 (212) stitches.

Next round Work even in pattern. Repeat last 2 rounds until 66 (68) stitches remain, switching to

smaller circular needle when needed. Remove markers. Work even in purl 1, knit 1 rib for 8" (20.5 cm).

FINISHING
Bind off loosely in rib. Weave in ends.

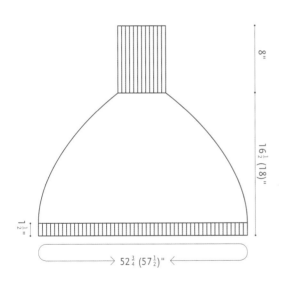

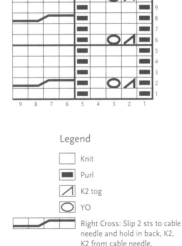

Legend

Knit

Purl

K2 tog

YO

Right Cross: Slip 2 sts to cable needle and hold in back, K2, K2 from cable needle.

PLEATS PLEASE

DESIGNED BY CATHY MAGUIRE

KNIT/INTERMEDIATE

The knife-pleat shaping in this classic poncho is both decorative and utilitarian. The pleats are knitted with a cable technique and decrease six stitches simultaneously.

SIZE
Circumference 16" (40.5 cm) at neck; 77" (195.5 cm) at lower edge
Length 15¼" (38.5 cm)

MATERIALS

 LION BRAND CASHMERE BLEND 72% MERINO, 15% NYLON, 13% CASHMERE
1.5 OZ (40 G) 84 YD (76 M) BALL

8 balls #098 Cream or color of your choice

• Size 10 (6 mm) knitting needles *or size to obtain gauge*

• Size 10 (6 mm) 16" (40.5 cm) circular needle

• Size 10 (6 mm) double-pointed needles

• Stitch holders

• Stitch marker

• Large-eyed, blunt needle

GAUGE
16 stitches + 24 rows = 4" (10 cm) in stockinette stitch (knit on right side, purl on wrong side).
Be sure to check your gauge.

STITCH EXPLANATIONS
RP (Right Pleat) Slip 3 stitches onto double-pointed needle, slip next 3 stitches onto 2nd double-pointed needle and turn to overlap first double-pointed needle in front. Turn remaining needle to overlap 2nd double-pointed needle in front. (There should now be 3 parallel needles forming a knife pleat with fold facing right.) *Knit 3 together, using 1 stitch from each of the 3 needles. Repeat from * 2 more times.
LP (Left Pleat) Slip 3 stitches onto double-pointed needle, slip next 3 stitches onto 2nd double-pointed needle and turn to overlap first

double-pointed needle in back. Turn remaining needle to overlap 2nd double-pointed needle in back. (There should now be 3 parallel needles forming a knife pleat with fold facing left.) *Knit 3 together, using 1 stitch from each of the 3 needles. Repeat from * 2 more times.

BACK

Cast on 78 stitches.

Rows 1 and 3 *Knit 2, purl 2; repeat from *, ending knit 2.

Rows 2 and 4 *Purl 2, knit 2; repeat from *, ending purl 2.

Rows 5–18 Work in stockinette stitch.

Row 19 (Pleat Row) Knit 2, RP, knit to last 11 stitches, LP, knit 2—66 stitches.

Rows 20–36 Work in stockinette stitch.

Row 37 (Pleat Row) Repeat Row 19—54 stitches.

Rows 38–54 Work in stockinette stitch.

Row 55 (Pleat Row) Repeat Row 19—42 stitches.

Rows 56–72 Work in stockinette stitch.

Row 73 (Pleat Row) Repeat Row 19—30 stitches.

Rows 74–90 Work in stockinette stitch.

Row 91 (Pleat Row) Repeat Row 19—18 stitches.

Row 92 (Shape Neck) Purl 3 and place these stitches on a holder, break yarn; place next 12 stitches on holder. Join yarn and purl last 3 stitches, place these 3 stitches on holder. Break yarn.

FRONT

Cast on 82 stitches.

Rows 1 and 3 *Knit 2, purl 2; repeat from *, ending knit 2.

Rows 2 and 4 *Purl 2, knit 2; repeat from *, ending purl 2.

Rows 5–18 Work in stockinette stitch.

Row 19 (Pleat Row) Knit 2, RP, knit to last 11 stitches, LP, knit 2—70 stitches.

Rows 20–36 Work in stockinette stitch.

Row 37 (Pleat Row) Repeat Row 19—58 stitches.

Rows 38–54 Work in stockinette stitch.

Row 55 (Pleat Row) Repeat Row 19—46 stitches.

Rows 56–72 Work in stockinette stitch.

Row 73 (Pleat Row) Repeat Row 19—34 stitches.

Rows 74–84 Work in stockinette stitch.

Row 85 (Pleat Row) Repeat Row 19—22 stitches.

Row 86 (Shape Neck) Purl 3, purl 2 together; place remaining 17 stitches on a holder.

Row 87 Knit 2 together, knit 2—3 stitches.

Row 88 Purl 1, purl 2 together—2 stitches.

Bind off.

Keeping center 12 stitches on holder, place remaining 5 stitches onto needle and knit 3, knit 2 together—4 stitches.

Next Row Purl 2 together, purl 2—3 stitches.

Next Row Knit 1, knit 2 together—2 stitches.

Bind off.

LEFT SIDE

Cast on 74 stitches.

Rows 1 and 3 *Knit 2, purl 2; repeat from *, ending knit 2.

Rows 2 and 4 *Purl 2, knit 2; repeat from *, ending purl 2.

Rows 5–18 Work in stockinette stitch.

Row 19 (Pleat Row) Knit 2, RP, knit to last 11 stitches, LP, knit 2—62 stitches.

Rows 20–36 Work in stockinette stitch.

Row 37 (Pleat Row) Repeat Row 19—50 stitches.

Rows 38–54 Work in stockinette stitch.

Row 55 (Pleat Row) Repeat Row 19—38 stitches.

Rows 56–72 Work in stockinette stitch.

Row 73 (Pleat Row) Repeat Row 19—26 stitches.

Rows 74–84 Work in stockinette stitch.

Row 85 (Pleat Row) Knit to last 11 stitches, LP, knit 2—20 stitches.

Row 86 Purl.

Row 87 Knit.

Row 88 (Shape Neck) Purl 7 and place these stitches on a holder, purl 2 together, purl 11—12 stitches.

Row 89 Knit.

Row 90 Purl 2 together, purl 10—11 stitches.

Row 91 Knit 2, RP—5 stitches.

Row 92 Purl 2 together, purl 3—4 stitches.

Place remaining 4 stitches on a 2nd holder.

RIGHT SIDE

Work as for Left Side through Row 84.

Row 85 (Pleat Row) Knit 2, RP, knit 15—20 stitches.

Row 86 Purl.

Row 87 (Shape Neck) Knit 7 and place these stitches on a holder, knit 2 together, knit 11—12 stitches.

Row 88 Purl.

Row 89 Knit 2 together, knit 10—11 stitches.

Row 90 Purl.

Row 91 Knit 2 together, LP—4 stitches.

Row 92 Purl.

Place remaining 4 stitches on a second holder.

FINISHING

Sew panels together.

NECK

With circular needle, beginning at the right neck edge of Back, knit 18 stitches from holder; across left Neck edge, knit 4 stitches from holder, pick up and knit 2 stitches, knit 7 stitches from holder; across the Front, pick up and knit 4 stitches, knit 12 stitches from holder, pick up and knit 4 stitches; across right Neck edge, knit 7 stitches from holder, pick up and knit 2 stitches, knit 4 stitches from holder—64 stitches. Place marker and join for working in the round. Work in knit 2, purl 2 rib for 14 rounds. Bind off. Weave in ends.

4.

PATTERNED WRAPS

Creativity comes in endless shapes and colors. The pieces in this chapter give you an opportunity to blend yarn colors and textures through a variety of knit and crochet techniques. Classic and reliable wraps like the poncho, the rebozo (a large rectangular wrap), and a cropped fitted poncho we call a "snuggle" make good backgrounds for colorwork techniques, including striping, patchwork knitting, Fair Isle stripes, and eye-catching granny squares. Sue Hunter has tapped ethnographic modes to create two colorfully crafted, his-and-hers blanket serapes. The Tweedy Circle Cape and the Town and Country Capelet are designed with irregular concentric stripes. Experiment with different palettes or textures. You'll find your own road to self-expression, and create something gorgeous along the way.

TOWN AND COUNTRY CAPELET

DESIGNED BY KIMBERLY KOTARY

CROCHET/EASY

Radiating rows of color are topped off with a luxuriant looped fringe and a contrasting suedelike collar in this sumptuous short cape that'll take you from city streets to country lanes.

SIZE

Width 16" (40.5 cm) at neck edge; 53" (134.5 cm) at lower edge
Length 15½" (39.5 cm)

MATERIALS

 LION BRAND LION SUEDE 100% POLYESTER 3 OZS (85 G) 122 YARDS (110 M) BALL

1 ball #126 Coffee (A) or color of your choice

 LION BRAND MOONLIGHT MOHAIR 35% MOHAIR, 30% ACRYLIC, 25% COTTON, 10% METALLIC POLYESTER 1.4 OZ (50 G) 82 YARDS (75 M) BALL

2 balls #204 Rainbow Falls (B), 2 balls #206 Purple Mountain (C), 3 balls #201 Rain Forest (E), or colors of your choice

• Size J-10 (6 mm) crochet hook *or size to obtain gauge*

• Large-eyed, blunt needle

GAUGE

12 single crochet + 12 rows = 4" (10 cm) with A.
12 double crochet + 6 rows = 4" (10 cm) with B.
Be sure to check your gauge.

STITCH EXPLANATION

2-double crochet shell 2 double crochet in same space.

NOTE

Cape is worked from the neck down in one piece, working in random stripes of Moonlight Mohair. Change color as desired.

COLLAR

Starting at top edge, with A, chain 49.
Row 1 (Wrong Side) Single crochet in 2nd chain from hook and in each chain across. Turn—48 single crochet.
Rows 2–7 Chain 1, single crochet in each stitch across. Turn.
Fasten off, leaving a long tail for sewing.

CAPE

Row 1 (Right Side) With right side facing, skip first 4 single crochet in Row 7 of Collar. Join desired color of Moonlight Mohair in next single crochet, chain 3, double crochet in each of next 39 single crochet. Turn, leaving remaining stitches unworked—40 stitches.
Row 2 Chain 3, double crochet in each of next 3 double crochet, *chain 1, double crochet in each of next 5 double crochet, chain 1, double crochet in each of next 4

double crochet; repeat from * across. Turn—40 double crochet; 8 chain 1-spaces.

Row 3 Chain 3, *double crochet in each double crochet across to next chain 1-space, 2-double crochet shell in next chain 1-space; repeat from * 7 more times, double crochet in each double crochet across. Turn—56 double crochet.

Row 4 Chain 3, *double crochet in each double crochet across to first double crochet of next shell, double crochet in first double crochet of shell, chain 1; repeat from * 7 more times, double crochet in each double crochet across. Turn—56 double crochet; 8 chain 1-spaces.

Rows 5–22 Repeat Rows 3–4, making 144 double crochet at end of Row 22.

Row 23 Repeat Row 3—160 double crochet. Fasten off.

LEFT FRONT TRIM

Row 1 With wrong side facing, join A in first skipped single crochet in Row 7 on left side of Collar (on Cape side of 4 skipped stitches), chain 1, single crochet in each single crochet across. Turn—4 single crochet.

Row 2 Chain 1, single crochet in each single crochet across. Turn. Repeat Row 2 until Trim measures 15" (38 cm) from bottom edge of Collar. Fasten off.

RIGHT FRONT TRIM

Row 1 With right side facing, join A in first skipped single crochet in Row 7 on right side of Collar (on Cape side of 4 skipped stitches), chain 1, single crochet in each single crochet across. Turn—4 single crochet.

Work as for Left Front Trim.

FINISHING

With large-eyed, blunt needle and A, sew Front Trims to adjacent edges of Cape.

TIE (MAKE 2)

With 2 strands of A held together, chain 30. Fasten off, leaving a tail. Tie tail to end of Row 6 of Collar. Weave in tail on other end of Tie. Make an overhand knot at end of Tie. Attach 2nd Tie to other side of Row 6 and complete as for first Tie. Weave in ends.

THE FLAPPER

DESIGNED BY GALINA CARROLL

KNIT/EASY

This simple, short poncho is full of surprising details; it blends unexpected colors imaginatively from the top down to its whimsical lower edge finish.

SIZE

Circumference 88" (223.5 cm) at lower edge
Length 12½" (32 cm), excluding Fringe

MATERIALS

 LION BRAND LANDSCAPES 50% WOOL, 50% ACRYLIC 1¾ OZ (50 G) 55 YD (50 M) BALL

2 balls each #271 Rose Garden (A), #273 Spring Desert (B), #279 Deep Sea (C), or colors of your choice

- Size 9 (5.5 mm) 24" (60 cm) circular needle *or size to obtain gauge*
- Size 9 (5.5 mm) double-pointed needles
- Stitch markers

GAUGE

10 stitches + 14 rounds = 4" (10 cm) in stockinette stitch (knit every round).

Be sure to check your gauge.

STRIPE PATTERN

Rounds 1–18 Work with A.
Rounds 19–34 Work with B.
Rounds 35–44 Work with C.

PONCHO

With A and circular needle, cast on 84 stitches. Place marker and join for working in the round, being careful not to twist.
Rounds 1–10 *Knit 1, purl 1; repeat from *.
Round 11 (Increase Round) *Knit 20, yarn over, place marker, knit 1, yarn over; repeat from * 3 more times—92 stitches.
Round 12 Knit.
Round 13 (Increase Round) *Knit to next marker, yarn over, slip marker, knit 1, yarn over; repeat from * 3 more times—100 stitches.
Round 14 Knit.

Rounds 15–44 Maintaining Stripe Pattern, repeat last 2 rounds—220 stitches at end of Round 44. Do not bind off.

FRINGE

Each Fringe panel is worked separately, with varying widths of 3–12 stitches, and varying lengths of 14–18 rows, at the knitter's discretion. Each Fringe panel is knit in C, with a few panels tipped in A at the knitter's discretion.
Panel 1 Knit 3 onto double-pointed needle. Turn; purl 3. Turn. Continue in stockinette stitch (knit on right side, purl on wrong side) on double-pointed needle for desired length. Bind off.
Panel 2 Join C and, using double-pointed needle, knit 5. Turn; purl 5. Turn. Continue in stockinette stitch to desired length. Bind off.
Continue working panels across bottom edge of Poncho. Weave in

TWEEDY CIRCLE CAPE

DESIGNED BY KIMBERLY KOTARY

KNIT/EASY

This semicircular cape is knit from the neck down in a gray scale of stripes. The contrasting suedelike collar and ties echo the velvet trim on vintage capes.

SIZE

Circumference 18" (45.5 cm) at neck; 113" (287 cm) at lower edge
Length 33" (84 cm)

MATERIALS

 LION BRAND LION SUEDE
100% POLYESTER
3 OZS (85 G) 122 YARDS (110 M) BALL

1 ball #153 Ebony (A) or color of your choice

 LION BRAND HOMESPUN
98% ACRYLIC, 2% POLYESTER
6 OZ (170 G) 185 YD (167 M) SKEIN

1 skein each #366 Metropolis (B), #343 Romanesque (C), #312 Edwardian (D), #300 Hepplewhite (E), or colors of your choice

- Size 9 (5.5 mm) 32" (81 cm) circular needle *or size to obtain gauge*
- Size 9 (5.5 mm) double-pointed needles *or size to obtain gauge*
- Stitch holders and stitch markers
- Large-eyed, blunt needle

GAUGE

12 stitches + 19 rows = 4" (10 cm) in stockinette stitch (knit on right side, purl on wrong side) with B. *Be sure to check your gauge.*

PATTERN STITCH

Seed stitch (even number of stitches)
Row 1 (Right Side) *K 1, purl 1; repeat from *.
Row 2 *Purl 1, knit 1; repeat from *.
Repeat Rows 1–2 for seed stitch.
Seed stitch (odd number of stitches)
Row 1 *K 1, purl 1; repeat from *, ending knit 1.
Repeat Row 1 for seed stitch.

NOTE

Cape is worked from the top down.

CAPE

With A, cast on 54 stitches. Work in seed stitch (even number of stitches) until piece measures 2½" (6.5 cm) from beginning, ending with a wrong side row. Place first 4 stitches on holder. Change to B. *Knit 8, place marker, knit 2, place marker, knit 7, place marker, knit 2, place marker; repeat from * once, knit 8, place last 4 stitches on holder.
Work 3 rows in stockinette stitch, beginning with a purl row.
Increase Row *Knit to marker, yarn over, slip marker, knit 2, slip marker, yarn over; repeat from * across, knit to end—8 stitches increased.
Repeat last 4 rows, randomly changing colors (B–E), until piece measures 32½" (82.5 cm) from beginning. Change to D and work 2 rows in knit 1, purl 1 rib. Bind off.

LEFT PLACKET

Slip 4 stitches from stitch holder at left front onto needle. With right side facing and A, knit 1, purl 1, knit 1, [purl 1, knit 1] into same stitch—5 stitches. Continue in seed stitch (odd number of stitches) until Placket measures 32½" (82.5 cm) from beginning. Bind off.

RIGHT PLACKET

Slip 4 stitches from stitch holder at right front onto needle. With right side facing and A, [knit 1, purl 1] into same stitch, knit 1, purl 1, knit 1—5 stitches. Continue in seed stitch (odd number of stitches) until Placket measures 32½" (82.5 cm) from beginning. Bind off.

I-CORD TIES

With A, double-pointed needle, and right side facing, pick up and knit 3 stitches at inside corner of collar. *Do not turn.* Slide stitches to other end of needle, carry yarn tightly behind work, and knit 3, working in the same direction. Repeat from * until Tie measures 17" (43 cm). Cut yarn and pull through stitches to secure. Repeat on opposite side of collar.

FINISHING

Sew Right and Left Plackets to Cape. Weave in ends.

ROSY GRANNY

DESIGNED BY KIMBERLY KOTARY

CROCHET/EASY

This beautiful wrap takes advantage of several shades of rose-colored wool-blend yarn. The pattern as written uses a different square pattern for the two end rows, but feel free to substitute the basic square if you prefer.

SIZE
25" wide x 70" long (63.5 x 178 cm)

MATERIALS

 LION BRAND WOOL-EASE
80% ACRYLIC, 20% WOOL
3 OZ (85 G) 197 YD (180 M) BALL

3 balls each #179 Chestnut Heather (A), #139 Dark Rose Heather (B), #140 Rose Heather (C), #104 Blush Heather (D), or colors of your choice

• Size J-10 (6 mm) crochet hook *or size to obtain gauge*

• Large-eyed, blunt needle

GAUGE
Each plain square = 5" x 5" (12.5 x 12.5 cm).
Be sure to check your gauge.

PLAIN SQUARE 1 (MAKE 30)
With A, chain 5. Join with slip stitch to form ring.

Round 1 (Right Side) Chain 3, 2 double crochet in ring, [chain 2, 3 double crochet in ring] 3 times, chain 2. Join with slip stitch in top of beginning chain. Fasten off A.

Round 2 (Wrong Side) With wrong side facing, join B in any chain 2-space, chain 3, [2 double crochet, chain 2, 3 double crochet] in same chain 2-space (corner made), chain 1, [3 double crochet, chain 2, 3 double crochet, chain 1] in each chain 2-space around. Join with slip stitch in top of beginning chain—4 corner chain 2-spaces. Fasten off B.

Round 3 (Right Side) With right side facing, join C in any chain 1-space, chain 3, 2 double crochet in same chain 1-space *chain 1, [3 double crochet, chain 2, 3 double crochet] in next chain 2-space, chain 1, 3 double crochet in next chain 1-space; repeat from * 2 more times, chain 1, [3 double crochet, chain 2, 3 double crochet] in next chain 2-space, chain 1. Join with slip stitch in top of beginning chain. Fasten off C.

Round 4 (Wrong Side) With wrong side facing, join D in first chain 1-space to the right of any corner chain 2-space, chain 3, 2 double crochet in same chain 1-space *chain 1, [3 double crochet, chain 2, 3 double crochet] in next corner chain 2-space, chain 1, [3 double crochet, chain 1] in each of next 2 chain 1-spaces; repeat from * 2 more times, [3 double crochet, chain 2, 3 double crochet] in next corner chain 2-space, chain 1, 3

double crochet in next chain 1-space, chain 1. Join with slip stitch in top of beginning chain. Fasten off D. Weave in ends.

PLAIN SQUARE 2 (MAKE 30)

Work as for Plain Square 1, working in the following color sequence: 1 round D, 1 round C, 1 round B, 1 round A.

FLOWER SQUARE 1 (MAKE 5)

With A, chain 5. Join with slip stitch to form ring.

Round 1 (Right Side) Chain 1, [single crochet, chain 4] 8 times in ring. Join with slip stitch in first single crochet—8 chain 4-spaces. Fasten off A.

Round 2 (Wrong Side) With wrong side facing, join B in any chain 4-space, chain 1, [single crochet, double crochet, tr, double crochet, single crochet, chain 1] in each chain 4-space around. Join with slip stitch in first single crochet. Turn—8 petals.

Round 3 (Right Side) Working behind petals, [chain 3, slip stitch] in each chain 1-space around—8 chain 3-spaces. Fasten off B.

Round 4 (Wrong Side) With wrong side facing, join C in any chain 3-space, chain 3, [2 double crochet, chain 2, 3 double crochet] in same chain 3-space, *chain 1, 3 double crochet in next chain 3-space, chain 1, [3 double crochet, chain 2, 3 double crochet] in next chain 3-space; repeat from * 2 more times, chain 1, 3 double crochet in next chain 3-space, chain 1. Join with slip stitch in top of beginning chain—4 corner chain 2-spaces. Fasten off C.

Round 5 (Wrong Side) With wrong side facing, join D in first chain 1-space to the right of any corner chain 2-space, chain 3, 2 double crochet in same chain 1-space, chain 1, *[3 double crochet, chain 2, 3 double crochet] in next corner chain 2-space, chain 1, [3 double crochet, chain 1] in each of next 2 chain 1-spaces; repeat from * 2 more times, [3 double crochet, chain 2, 3 double crochet] in next corner chain 2-space, chain 1, 3 double crochet in next chain 1-space, chain 1. Join with slip stitch in top of beginning chain. Fasten off D. Weave in ends.

FLOWER SQUARE 2 (MAKE 5)

Work as for Flower Square 1, working in the following color sequence: 1 round D, 2 rounds C, 1 round B, 1 round A.

FINISHING

Sew Plain Squares together, alternating Plain Squares 1 and 2 in a checkerboard pattern, 5 Squares across by 12 Squares long. Sew Flower Squares together, alternating Flower Squares 1 and 2 in two strips of 5 Squares. Sew a Flower Square strip to each end of the Plain Square piece.

EDGING

With right side facing, join A in any corner chain 2-space, chain 1, *[single crochet, chain 2, single crochet] in corner chain 2-space, single crochet in each double crochet and each chain-space across to next corner; repeat from * around. Join with slip stitch in first single crochet. Fasten off. Weave in ends.

MONCHO SERAPE

DESIGNED BY SUE HUNTER

KNIT/INTERMEDIATE

The serape is a traditional Mexican shawl, often brightly colored and fringed at the ends. The bold bands of color that are worked into this oversized blanket poncho are reminiscent of Southwestern loom-woven blankets. Make this one as a labor of love for the man in your life.

SIZE

Width 60" (152.5 cm)
Length 31" (79 cm)

MATERIALS

 LION BRAND WOOL-EASE
80% ACRYLIC, 20% WOOL
3 OZ (85 G) 197 YD (180 M) BALL

4 balls #152 Oxford Grey (A), 1 ball #151 Grey Heather (B), 2 balls #115 Blue Mist (C), 1 ball #130 Green Heather (D), 5 balls #153 Black (E), 1 ball #138 Cranberry (F), 1 ball #179 Chestnut Heather (G), or colors of your choice

- Size 8 (5 mm) 29" (74 cm) circular needle *or size to obtain gauge*

- Stitch holders

GAUGE

18 stitches + 24 rows = 4" (10 cm) in stockinette stitch (knit on right side, purl on wrong side).
Be sure to check your gauge.

STITCH EXPLANATION

M1 (make 1 stitch) An increase worked by lifting the horizontal thread lying between the needles and placing it onto the left needle. Work this new stitch through the back loop.

NOTE

Poncho is worked in one piece from side to side.

PONCHO

With A, cast on 98 stitches. Work 8 rows in garter stitch (knit every row). Change to stockinette stitch, changing colors as follows: 2 rows A, 1 row B, 1 row C, 1 row D, 1 row B, 2 rows A, 5 rows C, 1 row E.
Next Row (Increase Row) With E, *k 7, M1; repeat from *—112 stitches.

Continue in stockinette stitch, changing colors as follows: 5 rows C, 1 row F, 2 rows E, 3 rows G, 1 row B, 2 rows A, 1 row D, 1 row E, 1 row C, 2 rows A, 1 row B, 1 row G.
Next Row (Increase Row) With G, *k 4, M1; repeat from *—140 stitches. Continue in stockinette stitch, changing colors as follows: 1 row G, 2 rows E, 1 row F, 7 rows A.

INTARSIA SECTION

Row 1 With A, knit 4, *join small ball of E and knit 6, join small ball of A and knit 8; repeat from *, ending by joining small ball of E and knit 6, join small ball of A and knit 4.
Rows 2, 4, and 6 With A, purl 4; *with E, purl 6; with A, purl 8; repeat from *, ending with E, purl 6; with A, purl 4.

Rows 3 and 5 With A, knit 4; *with E, knit 6; with A, knit 8; repeat from *, ending with E, knit 6; with A, knit 4.

Work 2 rows in stockinette stitch with A.

Next Row (Increase Row) With A, *k 5, M1; repeat from *—168 stitches. Continue in stockinette stitch, changing colors as follows: 4 rows A, 10 rows E, 2 rows F, 1 row E.

Next Row (Increase Row) With E, *k 6, M1; repeat from *—196 stitches. Continue in stockinette stitch, changing colors as follows: 8 rows E, 2 rows A, 1 row B, 1 row C, 1 row D, 1 row B, 1 row A.

Next Row (Increase Row) With A, *k 7, M1; repeat from *—224 stitches. Continue in stockinette stitch, changing colors as follows: 5 rows C, 2 rows E, 2 rows C.

Next Row (Increase Row) With C, *k 8, M1; repeat from *—252 stitches. Continue in stockinette stitch, changing colors as follows: 2 rows C, 1 row F, 2 rows E, 3 rows G, 1 row B, 2 rows A, 1 row D, 1 row E, 1 row C, 2 rows A, 1 row B.

Next Row (Increase Row) With G, *k 9, M1; repeat from *—280 stitches. Continue in stockinette stitch, changing colors as follows: 2 rows G, 2 rows E, 1 row F, 7 rows A.

Row 1 With A, purl 4, *join small ball of E and purl 6, join small ball of A and purl 8; repeat from *, ending by joining small ball of E and purl 6, join small ball of A and purl 4.

Rows 2, 4, and 6 With A, knit 4; *with E, knit 6; with A, knit 8; repeat from *, ending with E, knit 6; with A, knit 4.

Rows 3 and 5 With A, purl 4; *with E, purl 6; with A, purl 8; repeat from *, ending with E, purl 6; with A, purl 4.

Continue in stockinette stitch, changing colors as follows: 7 rows A, 12 rows E, 1 row F, 1 row B, 1 row F, 1 row E.

Next Row With E, knit 135, knit 2 together, place remaining 143 stitches on holder for Back—136 stitches for Right Front.

RIGHT FRONT

With E, work 9 rows in stockinette stitch, decrease 1 stitch at neck edge every row—127 stitches. Work 8 rows in garter stitch. Bind off.

LEFT FRONT

With E, cast on 127 stitches. Work 8 rows in garter stitch. Work 10 rows in stockinette stitch, increase 1 stitch at neck edge every row—137 stitches. Place stitches on 2nd holder for Left Front.

BACK

Place stitches from first holder onto needle. Join new ball of E and knit across—143 stitches. Continue in stockinette stitch, changing colors as follows: 15 rows E, 2 rows F, 1 row B, 1 row A, 1 row E, 1 row A, 1 row B, 2 rows F, 16 rows E.

JOIN BACK AND LEFT FRONT

With E, purl across row and then across stitches from holder—280 stitches.

Continue in stockinette stitch, changing colors as follows: 1 row F, 1 row B, 1 row F, 12 rows E, 7 rows A.

Row 1 With A, knit 4, *join small ball of E and knit 6, join small ball of A and knit 8; repeat from *, ending by joining small ball of E and knit 6, join small ball of A and knit 4.

Rows 2, 4, and 6 With A, purl 4; *with E, purl 6; with A, purl 8; repeat from *, ending with E, purl 6; with A, purl 4.

Rows 3 and 5 With A, knit 4; *with E, knit 6; with A, knit 8; repeat from *, ending with E, knit 6; with A, knit 4.

Continue in stockinette stitch, changing colors as follows: 7 rows A, 1 row F, 2 rows E, 2 rows G.

Next Row (Decrease Row) With G, *k 8, knit 2 together; repeat from *—252 stitches.

Continue in stockinette stitch, changing colors as follows: 1 row B, 2 rows A, 1 row C, 1 row E, 1 row D, 2 rows A, 1 row B, 3 rows G, 2 rows E, 1 row F, 2 rows C.

Next Row (Decrease Row) With C, *k 7, knit 2 together; repeat from *—224 stitches.

Continue in stockinette stitch, changing colors as follows: 2 rows C, 2 rows E, 5 rows C.

Next Row (Decrease Row) With A, *k 6, knit 2 together; repeat from *—196 stitches.

Continue in stockinette stitch, changing colors as follows: 1 row A, 1 row B, 1 row D, 1 row C, 1 row B, 2 rows A, 6 rows E.

Next Row (Decrease Row) With E, *k 5, knit 2 together; repeat from *—168 stitches.

Continue in stockinette stitch, changing colors as follows: 3 rows E, 2 rows F, 10 rows E, 4 rows A.

Next Row (Decrease Row) With A, *k 4, knit 2 together; repeat from *—140 stitches.

Work 2 rows in stockinette stitch with A.

INTARSIA SECTION

Row 1 With A, purl 4, *join small ball of E and purl 6, join small ball of A and purl 8; repeat from *, ending by joining small ball of E and purl 6, join small ball of A and purl 4.

Rows 2, 4, and 6 With A, knit 4; *with E, knit 6; with A, knit 8; repeat from *, ending with E, knit 6; with A, knit 4.

Rows 3 and 5 With A, purl 4; *with E, purl 6; with A, purl 8; repeat from *, ending with E, purl 6; with A, purl 4.

Continue in stockinette stitch, changing colors as follows: 7 rows A, 1 row F, 2 rows E, 1 row G.

Next Row (Decrease Row) With G, *k 3, knit 2 together; repeat from *—112 stitches.

Continue in stockinette stitch, changing colors as follows: 1 row G, 1 row B, 2 rows A, 1 row C, 1 row E, 1 row D, 2 rows A, 1 row B, 3 rows G, 2 rows E, 1 row F, 5 rows C.

Next Row (Decrease Row) With E, *k 6, knit 2 together; repeat from *—98 stitches.

Continue in stockinette stitch, changing colors as follows: 1 row E, 5 rows C, 2 rows A, 1 row B, 1 row D, 1 row C, 1 row B, 2 rows A. Work 8 rows in garter stitch. Bind off. Weave in ends.

SERAPE WRAP

DESIGNED BY SUE HUNTER

KNIT/INTERMEDIATE

Traditionally worn in Mexico, a serape is the wearer's constant companion and a versatile garment for both day and night. Urban cowgirls will find comfort and satisfaction in making and wearing this colorful wrap.

SIZE
Width 53" (134.5 cm)
Length 24¾" (63 cm)

MATERIALS

 LION BRAND WOOL-EASE
80% ACRYLIC, 20% WOOL
3 OZ (85 G) 197 YD (180 M) BALL

3 balls each #126 Chocolate Brown (A), #125 Camel (B). 1 ball each #146 Lilac (C), #147 Purple (D), #139 Dark Rose Heather (E), #179 Chestnut Heather (F), #127 Mink Brown (G), or colors of your choice

• Size 8 (5 mm) 29" (74 cm) circular needle *or size to obtain gauge*

• Stitch holders

GAUGE

18 stitches + 24 rows = 4" (10 cm) in stockinette stitch (knit on right side, purl on wrong side).
Be sure to check your gauge.

STITCH EXPLANATION

M1 (make 1 stitch) An increase worked by lifting the horizontal thread lying between the needles and placing it onto the left needle. Work this new stitch through the back loop.

NOTE

Poncho is worked in one piece from side to side.

PONCHO

With A, cast on 78 stitches. Work 8 rows in garter stitch (knit every row). Change to stockinette stitch, changing colors as follows: 2 rows B, 1 row C, 1 row D, 1 row E, 1 row C.

Next Row (Increase Row) With B, *k 6, M1; repeat from *—91 stitches. Continue in stockinette stitch, changing colors as follows: 1 row B, 5 rows E, 2 rows A, 3 rows E.

Next Row (Increase Row) With E, *k 7, M1; repeat from *—104 stitches. Continue in stockinette stitch, changing colors as follows: 1 row E, 1 row F, 2 rows A, 3 rows G, 1 row C, 2 rows B, 1 row D, 1 row A, 1 row E, 2 rows B, 1 row C, 1 row G.

Next Row (Increase Row) With G, *k 4, M1; repeat from *—130 stitches. Continue in stockinette stitch, changing colors as follows: 1 row G, 2 rows A, 1 row F, 7 rows B.

INTARSIA SECTION

Row 1 With B, knit 4, *join small ball of A and knit 5, join small ball of B and knit 4; repeat from *.

Rows 2, 4, and 6 With B, purl 4; *with A, purl 5; with B, purl 4; repeat from *.

Rows 3 and 5 With B, knit 4; *with A, knit 5; with B, knit 4; repeat from *.

Work 4 rows in stockinette stitch with B.

Next Row (Increase Row) With B, *k 5, M1; repeat from *—156 stitches. Continue in stockinette stitch, changing colors as follows: 2 rows B, 10 rows A, 2 rows F, 5 rows A.

Next Row (Increase Row) With A, *k 6, M1; repeat from *—182 stitches. Continue in stockinette stitch, changing colors as follows: 4 rows A, 1 row F, 2 rows A, 3 rows G, 1 row C, 2 rows B, 1 row D, 1 row A, 1 row E, 2 rows B, 1 row C, 2 rows G.

Next Row (Increase Row) With G, *k 7, M1; repeat from *—208 stitches. Continue in stockinette stitch, changing colors as follows: 2 rows A, 1 row F, 8 rows B.

Next Row (Increase Row) With B, *k 13, M1; repeat from *—224 stitches. Continue in stockinette stitch, changing colors as follows: 1 row B, 1 row E, 1 row C, 1 row E, 20 rows B, 1 row E, 1 row C, 1 row E, 2 rows B.

Next Row With B, knit 104, knit 2 together, place remaining 118 stitches on holder for Back—105 stitches for Right Front.

RIGHT FRONT

With B, work 7 rows in stockinette stitch, decrease 1 stitch at neck edge every row—98 stitches. Work 8 rows in garter stitch. Bind off.

LEFT FRONT

With B, cast on 98 stitches and work 8 rows in garter stitch. Work 8 rows in stockinette stitch, increase 1 stitch at neck edge every row—106 stitches. Place stitches on second holder for Left Front.

BACK

Place stitches from first stitch holder onto needle. Join new ball of B and knit across—118 stitches. Continue in stockinette stitch, changing colors as follows: 12 rows B, 2 rows E, 1 row C, 1 row D, 1 row B, 1 row D, 1 row C, 2 rows E, 13 rows B.

JOIN BACK AND LEFT FRONT

With B, purl across row and then across stitches from holder—224 stitches.

Continue in stockinette stitch, changing colors as follows: 1 row B, 1 row E, 1 row C, 1 row E, 20 rows B, 1 row E, 1 row C, 1 row E, 3 rows B.

Next Row (Decrease Row) With B, *k 12, knit 2 together; repeat from *—208 stitches.

Continue in stockinette stitch, changing colors as follows: 6 rows B, 1 row F, 2 rows A, 2 rows G.

Next Row (Decrease Row) With G, *k 6, knit 2 together; repeat from *—182 stitches.

Continue in stockinette stitch, changing colors as follows: 1 row C, 2 rows B, 1 row E, 1 row A, 1 row D, 2 rows B, 1 row C, 3 rows G, 2 rows A, 1 row F, 6 rows A.

Next Row (Decrease Row) With A, *k 5, knit 2 together; repeat from *—156 stitches.

Continue in stockinette stitch, changing colors as follows: 3 rows A, 2 rows F, 10 rows A, 4 rows B.

Next Row (Decrease Row) With B, *k 4, knit 2 together; repeat from *—130 stitches.

Work 2 rows in stockinette stitch with B.

INTARSIA SECTION

Row 1 With B, purl 4, *join small ball of A and purl 5, join small ball of B and purl 4; repeat from *.

Rows 2, 4, and 6 With B, knit 4; *with A, knit 5; with B, knit 4; repeat from *.

Rows 3 and 5 With B, purl 4; *with A, purl 5; with B, purl 4; repeat from *.

Continue in stockinette stitch, changing colors as follows: 7 rows B, 1 row F, 2 rows A, 1 row G.

Next Row (Decrease Row) With G, *k 3, knit 2 together; repeat from *—104 stitches.

Continue in stockinette stitch, changing colors as follows: 1 row G, 1 row C, 2 rows B, 1 row E, 1 row A, 1 row D, 2 rows B, 1 row C, 3 rows G, 2 rows A, 1 row F, 1 row E.

Next Row (Decrease Row) With E, *k 6, knit 2 together; repeat from *—91 stitches.

Continue in stockinette stitch, changing colors as follows: 3 rows E, 2 rows A, 5 rows E, 1 row B.

Next Row (Decrease Row) With B, *k 5, knit 2 together; repeat from *—78 stitches.

Continue in stockinette stitch, changing colors as follows: 1 row C, 1 row E, 1 row D, 1 row C, 2 rows B.

FINISHING

With A, work 8 rows in garter stitch. Bind off. Weave in ends.

SERAPE WRAP

LUSH GRANNY

DESIGNED BY KATHERINE ENG

CROCHET/INTERMEDIATE

A little creative thinking is all it takes to transform a granny square wrap into a luxurious and opulent fashion accessory. The metallic mohair yarn adds a dazzling splash.

SIZE
Width 13½" (34.5 cm)
Length 67½" (171.5 cm)

MATERIALS

LION BRAND LION SUEDE
100% POLYESTER
3 OZ (85 G) 122 YD (110 M) BALL

3 balls #146 Fuchsia (A), 2 balls #133 Spice (B), or colors of your choice

LION BRAND MOONLIGHT
MOHAIR 35% MOHAIR, 30% ACRYLIC, 25% COTTON, 10% METALLIC POLYESTER
1¾ OZ (50 G) 82 YD (75 M) BALL

2 balls #207 Coral Reef (c) or color of your choice

- Size G-6 (4 mm) crochet hook *or size to obtain gauge*

- Size H-8 (5 mm) crochet hook *or size to obtain gauge*

GAUGE
Round 1 of Square 1 = 2¼" (5.5 cm) across.
Square 1 = 4½" x 4½" (11.5 x 11.5 cm).
Be sure to check your gauge.

STITCH EXPLANATION
FPtr (front post triple crochet) Yarn over twice, working from front to back to front, insert hook around post of stitch of row below, yarn over and draw up a loop, [yarn over and draw through 2 loops on hook] 3 times. Skip stitch behind the front post triple crochet.

SQUARE 1
With smaller hook and B, chain 3. Join with slip stitch to form ring.
Round 1 (Right Side) Chain 3, 2 double crochet in ring, chain 2,

[3 double crochet, chain 2] 3 times in ring. Join with slip stitch in top of beginning chain—4 corner chain 2-spaces. Fasten off B.

Round 2 With right side facing and larger hook, join A in any corner chain 2-space, chain 1, *[single crochet, chain 2, single crochet] in chain 2-space, single crochet in each of next 3 double crochet; repeat from * around. Join with slip stitch in first single crochet—4 corner chain 2-spaces. Fasten off A.

Round 3 With right side facing, join C in any corner chain 2-space, chain 1, *[single crochet, chain 2, single crochet] in chain 2-space, chain 1, skip next single crochet, single crochet in next single crochet, working in front of last round, FPtr around the post of next corresponding double crochet 2 rounds below, skip single crochet behind FPtr crochet just made, single crochet in next single crochet, chain 1, skip next single crochet; repeat from * around. Join with slip stitch in first single crochet—4 corner chain 2-spaces. Fasten off C.

Round 4 With right side facing, join B in any corner chain 2-space, chain 1, *[single crochet, chain 4, single crochet] in corner chain 2-space, chain 1, [single crochet, chain 2, single crochet] in next chain 1-space, [single crochet, chain 2, single crochet] in next front post triple crochet, [single crochet, chain 2, single crochet] in next chain 1-space, chain 1; repeat from * around. Join with slip stitch in first single crochet—4 corner chain 4-loops; 3 chain 2-spaces on each side. Fasten off.

SQUARE 2

Work as for Square 1 in the following color sequence: 1 round A, 1 round B, 1 round C, 1 round A. Join to previous square while working Round 4 as follows:

Round 4 (Joining Round) Work as for Round 4 of Square 1, joining to previous square in each chain 4-loop and each chain 2-space on 1 side as follows: to join chain 4-loops, work chain 2, drop loop from hook, insert hook from front to back in corresponding chain 4-loop of previous square, pick up dropped loop, chain 2. To join chain 2-spaces, work chain 1, drop loop from hook, insert hook from front to back in corresponding chain 2-space of previous square, pick up dropped loop, chain 1.

Make and join 22 more of Square 1, and 21 more of Square 2, in a rectangle, 3 wide by 15 long, alternating squares 1 and 2 throughout. Join each square to previous squares as for Square 2. To join where 4 corners meet, chain 2, drop loop from hook, insert hook from front to back in next corresponding chain 4-loop of previous square, chain 1, drop loop, skip next chain 4-loop on opposite side, draw dropped loop through next chain 4-loop on next square, chain 2, and continue around.

BORDER

Round 1 With right side of wrap facing, join A in chain 2-space to the left of any corner chain 4-loop, chain 1, *[single crochet, chain 2, single crochet] in each chain 2-space and each chain 4-loop at junctions across to next corner, [single crochet, chain 2, single crochet, chain 2, single crochet, chain 2, single crochet] in corner chain 4-loop; repeat from * around. Join with slip stitch in first single crochet.

FINISHING

Fasten off. Weave in ends.

SHOULDER SNUGGLE

DESIGNED BY CATHY MAGUIRE

KNIT/INTERMEDIATE

Stripes of stockinette, garter stitch, ribbing, and simple Fair Isle patterning blend two deluxe yarns to keep you snug as a bug. Splashes of rich color lend an air of bohemian chic.

SIZE

Circumference 24" (61 cm) at neck; 48" (122 cm) at lower edge
Length 10" (25.5 cm)

MATERIALS

LION BRAND LION SUEDE
100% POLYESTER
3 OZ (85 G) 122 YD (110 M) BALL

1 ball each #126 Coffee (A), #146 Fuchsia (B), #178 Teal (C), #147 Eggplant (D), #189 Garnet (E), or colors of your choice

LION BRAND MOONLIGHT MOHAIR 35% MOHAIR, 30% ACRYLIC, 25% COTTON, 10% METALLIC POLYESTER
1¾ OZ (50 G) 82 YD (75 M) BALL

1 ball #203 Safari (F) or color of your choice

• Size 9 (5.5 mm) 29" (70 cm) circular needle *or size to obtain gauge*

• Stitch marker

GAUGE

12 stitches + 18 rounds = 4" (10 cm) in stockinette stitch (knit every round) with A.
Be sure to check your gauge.

MINI PONCHO

With A, cast on 144 stitches. Place marker and join for working in the round.
Rounds 1–3 [Knit 2, purl 2] around. Break off A and join B.
Rounds 4–5 Purl. Break off B and join C.
Round 6 Knit. Break off C and join D.
Rounds 7–8 Knit. Break off D and join E.
Round 9 Knit. Break off E and join A.
Rounds 10–11 [Knit 1, purl 1] around. Break off A and join F.
Round 12 Knit. Break off F and join B.
Round 13 Knit. Break off B and join D.
Round 14 Knit. Break off D and join C.
Round 15 Knit. Break off C and join A.
Round 16 Knit. Break off A and join E.
Round 17 Knit. Join F.

FAIR ISLE SECTION 1

Round 18 *Knit 2 with E, knit 1 with F; repeat from * around.
Round 19 *Knit 1 with E, knit 2 with F; repeat from * around. Break off E.
Round 20 Knit. Break off F and join A.
Round 21 Knit.
Rounds 22–23 [Knit 2, purl 2] around. After Round 23, break off A and join B and C.

FAIR ISLE SECTION 2

Round 24 *Knit 3 with B, knit 3 with C; repeat from * around.
Round 25 *Knit 1 with B, knit 1 with C; repeat from * around.

Round 26 Repeat Round 24. Break off both B and C, and join E.
Rounds 27–28 Knit. After Round 28, break off E and join F.
Round 29 Knit. Break off F and join E.
Rounds 30–31 Knit. After Round 31, break off E and join A and D.

FAIR ISLE SECTION 3
Round 32 *Knit 6 with A, knit 6 with D; repeat from * around. Join F.
Round 33 (Decrease Round) *Knit 2 with A, knit 2 together with F, knit 2 with A, knit 2 with D, knit 2 together with F, knit 2 with D; repeat from * around—120 stitches. Break off F.
Round 34 *Knit 5 with A, knit 5 with D; repeat from * around. Break off A and D, and join B.
Rounds 35–38 Work in garter stitch [knit 1 round, purl 1 round]. After Round 38, break off B and join F.
Rounds 39–42 Work in garter stitch. After Round 42, break off F and join E.
Rounds 43–44 Work in garter stitch.
Round 45 (Decrease Round) *Knit 3, knit 2 together; repeat from * around—96 stitches.

Round 46 Work in garter stitch. Break off E and join F.
Rounds 47 Work in garter stitch.
Round 48 (Decrease Round) *Knit 2, knit 2 together; repeat from * around—72 stitches.
Rounds 49–50 Work in garter stitch.

After Round 50, break off F and join A.
Rounds 51–56 Work in garter stitch.

FINISHING
Bind off all stitches. Weave in ends.

SHOULDER SNUGGLE

5.
DRESSY WRAPS

Luxurious and glitzy yarns are fashioned to make wraps with stunning textures in both knit and crochet. Nostalgia for old-world romance is reflected in Stole My Heart and Victorian Capelet; both designs embrace the texture of a metallic mohair yarn to bring out your softer side. The Bowtie Wrap, and the Mesh Poncho, with its funky bead-trimmed fringe, are perfect cover-ups for a night on the town.

VICTORIAN CAPELET

DESIGNED BY VLADIMIR TERIOKHIN

KNIT/EASY

Both ladylike and dramatic, this capelet is easy to knit and works up quickly in super bulky yarn.

SIZE

Width 31" (78.5 cm) at lower edge
Length 15¼" (38.5 cm)

MATERIALS

 LION BRAND CHENILLE THICK & QUICK 91% ACRYLIC, 9% RAYON 100 YD (90 M) SKEIN

2 skeins #147 Purple (main color) or color of your choice

 LION BRAND MOONLIGHT MOHAIR 35% MOHAIR, 30% ACRYLIC, 25% COTTON, 10% METALLIC POLYESTER 1¾ OZ (50 G) 82 YD (75 M) BALL

1 ball #206 Purple Mountain (contrasting color) or color of your choice

• Size 10.5 (6.5 mm) 36" (91 cm) circular needle *or size to obtain gauge*

• Stitch holders

• Stitch markers

• Large-eyed, blunt needle

GAUGE

10 stitches + 13 rows = 4" (10 cm) in stockinette stitch (knit on right side, purl on wrong side) with main color.
Be sure to check your gauge.

YOKE

With main color, cast on 23 stitches using backward loop method. Purl 1 row. Working in stockinette stitch, cast on 2 stitches at beginning of next 4 rows, then 1 stitch at beginning of following 4 rows—35 stitches. Knit 10; place remaining 25 stitches on holder.

RIGHT SHOULDER

Rows 1–5 Work in stockinette stitch.
Row 6 (Right Side) Knit 10, cast on 8 stitches—18 stitches.

Rows 7, 9, 11, and 13 Purl 2, knit 1, purl 1, knit 1, purl to end of row.
Rows 8 and 10 Bind off 1 stitch, knit to last 5 stitches, purl 1, knit 1, purl 1, knit 2.
Rows 12 and 14 Bind off 2 stitches, knit to last 5 stitches, purl 1, knit 1, purl 1, knit 2.
Row 15 Purl 2, knit 1, purl 1, knit 1, purl to end of row.
Place these 12 stitches on holder.

LEFT SHOULDER

With right side facing, place 25 stitches from holder onto needle and join main color.
Row 1 (Right Side) Bind off 15 stitches for Back neck, knit to end of row—10 stitches.
Rows 2–5 Work in stockinette stitch.
Row 6 Purl 10, cast on 8 stitches—18 stitches.
Rows 7, 9, 11, and 13 Knit 2, purl 1, knit 1, purl 1, knit to end of row.

Rows 8 and 10 Bind off 1 stitch, purl to last 5 stitches, knit 1, purl 1, knit 1, purl 2.

Rows 12 and 14 Bind off 2 stitches, purl to last 5 stitches, knit 1, purl 1, knit 1, purl 2.

Row 15 Knit 2, purl 1, knit 1, purl 1, knit to end of row—12 stitches.

Row 16 Purl to last 5 stitches, knit 1, purl 1, knit 1, purl 2. Do not break yarn.

BODY

Row 1 Knit 2, purl 1, knit 1, purl 1, knit 7; pick up and knit 19 stitches evenly spaced around Left Shoulder; pick up and knit 23 stitches across cast-on edge; pick up and knit 19 stitches evenly spaced around Right Shoulder. From holder knit 7, purl 1, knit 1, purl 1, knit 2—85 stitches.

Row 2 Purl 2, knit 1, purl 1, knit 1, purl 7; place marker, purl 5, place marker; purl 10; place marker, purl 5, place marker; purl 21; place marker, purl 5, place marker; purl 10; place marker, purl 5, place marker; purl 7, knit 1, purl 1, knit 1, purl 2.

SHAPE BODY

Increase Row Knit 2, purl 1, knit 1, purl 1, *k to next marker, knit into back and front of next stitch, knit to 1 stitch before marker, knit into front and back of next stitch; repeat from * 3 more times, knit to last 5 stitches, purl 1, knit 1, purl 1, knit 2—93 stitches.

Continuing in stockinette stitch, repeat increase row every 4th row 9 times total—157 stitches.

Keeping first and last 5 stitches in pattern, work 7 rows in garter stitch (knit every row), ending with a right side row. Bind off.

COLLAR

BACK

With wrong side of capelet facing and main color, pick up and knit 10 stitches across Back neck. Working in garter stitch, increase 1 stitch each end every 3rd row 4 times—18 stitches. Work even in garter stitch until Collar Back measures 6" (15 cm). Bind off all stitches.

SIDES

With wrong side of capelet facing and main color, pick up and knit 12 stitches evenly spaced along side edge of Collar Back. Working in garter stitch, decrease 1 stitch at neck edge every other row until 1 stitch remains. Fasten off. Repeat on other side.

RUFFLE

With right side of Collar facing and contrasting color, pick up and knit 85 stitches evenly spaced across Collar edge.

Rows 1, 3, 5, 7, and 9 (Wrong Side) Knit 2, purl to last 2 stitches, knit 2.

Row 2 Knit 3, yarn over, [knit 4, yarn over, knit 1, yarn over] 15 times, knit 4, yarn over, knit 3—117 stitches.

Row 4 Knit 3, yarn over, [knit 6, yarn over, knit 1, yarn over] 15 times, knit 6, yarn over, knit 3—149 stitches.

Row 6 Knit 3, yarn over, [knit 8, yarn over, knit 1, yarn over] 15 times, knit 8, yarn over, knit 3—181 stitches.

Row 8 Knit 3, yarn over, [knit 10, yarn over, knit 1, yarn over] 15 times, knit 10, yarn over, knit 3—213 stitches.

Row 10 Purl.

FINISHING

Bind off all stitches as if to purl. Weave in ends.

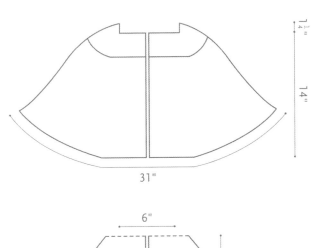

14"

7 1/4"

31"

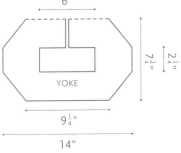

6"

2 1/4"
7 3/4"

YOKE

9 1/4"

14"

STOLE MY HEART

DESIGNED BY MARIE HONAN

KNIT/INTERMEDIATE

You'll be smitten with this romantic lace stole from the moment you cast on . Nostalgia for old-world romance is reflected in the feminine shape and softness of the knitted lace.

SIZE
Width 16" (40.5 cm)
Length 64" (162.5 cm)

MATERIALS

 LION BRAND MOONLIGHT MOHAIR
35% MOHAIR, 30% ACRYLIC, 25% COTTON, 10% METALLIC POLYESTER
1¾ OZ (50 G) 82 YD (75 M) BALL

8 balls #203 Safari or color of your choice

- Size 10 (6 mm) knitting needles *or size to obtain gauge*

- Size 10.5 (6.5 mm) double-pointed needles

- Stitch holder

- Large-eyed, blunt needle

GAUGE
15.25 stitches + 21 rows = 4" (10 cm) in pattern on smaller needles. *Be sure to check your gauge.*

STITCH EXPLANATIONS

M1 (make 1 stitch) An increase worked by lifting the horizontal thread lying between the needles and placing it onto the left needle. Work this new stitch through the back loop.

Grafting Holding the 2 needles parallel with wrong sides of fabric together, thread a large-eyed, blunt needle with one of the yarn ends and work as follows: Insert needle as if to purl into first stitch on front piece. Insert needle as if to knit into first stitch on back piece. Then follow steps 1–4 as outlined below. **Step 1** Insert needle as if to knit through first stitch on front needle and let the stitch drop from the needle. **Step 2** Insert needle into 2nd stitch on front needle as if to purl and pull the yarn through, leaving stitch on the needle. **Step 3** Insert needle into first stitch on back needle as if to purl and let it drop from the needle. **Step 4** Then insert it as if to knit through 2nd stitch on back needle and pull the yarn through, leaving stitch on the needle. Repeat steps 1–4 until all stitches are gone. When finished, adjust tension as necessary. Weave in ends.

STOLE

With smaller needles, cast on 61 stitches.

Row 1 Knit 3, *yarn over, knit 2, purl 3 together, knit 2, yarn over, knit 1; repeat from * to last 2 stitches, knit 2.

Row 2 Purl.

Rows 3–6 Repeat Rows 1–2.

Row 7 Knit 2, purl 2 together, *knit 2, yarn over, knit 1, yarn over, knit 2, purl 3 together; repeat from * to last 9 stitches, knit 2, yarn over, knit 1, yarn over, knit 2, purl 2 together, knit 2.

Row 8 Purl.

Rows 9–12 Repeat Rows 7–8.
Work Rows 1–12 of pattern 4
more times.

DIVIDE FOR OPENING

With right side facing, divide
stitches between 2 double-pointed
needles by slipping the first stitch
onto needle 1, the 2nd stitch onto
needle 2, the 3rd stitch onto needle
1, the 4th stitch onto needle 2,
and so on until you have 31
stitches on needle 1 and 30
stitches on needle 2.
Work each set of stitches separately. With right side facing and
stitches on needle 1, work 2 rows
stockinette stitch, decrease 2
stitches evenly spaced across first
row—29 stitches. Work 30 rows in
pattern. Break yarn, leaving stitches
on needle.

With right side facing and stitches
on needle 2, join yarn and work 2
rows stockinette stitch, decrease 1
stitch at center of first row—29
stitches. Work 30 rows in pattern.
Do not break yarn.

CLOSE OPENING

With wrong side facing, transfer
stitches back to smaller needle by
slipping first stitch from needle 1,
then next stitch from needle 2 and
so on—58 stitches. The working
yarn should be at the tip of the
needle, ready to be worked.
Work 78 rows in pattern, increasing
3 stitches evenly spaced across
first row as follows: Knit 2, M1,
[yarn over, knit 2, purl 3 together,
knit 2, yarn over, knit 1] 3 times,
yarn over, knit 2, purl 2 together,
knit 2, yarn over, knit 1, [yarn over,
knit 2, purl 3 together, knit 2, yarn
over, knit 1] 3 times, M1, knit 1—
61 stitches. Place stitches on
holder.
Make second side as for first.

FINISHING

Graft the 2 sides together. Weave
in ends. Steam lightly to desired
shape. Moonlight Mohair machine
washes, so the following method
works well: put Stole in your
washer and fill with a couple of
inches of cool water. Thoroughly
wet Stole by gently squeezing in
the water. Spin briefly until just
damp. Lay the damp Stole on
towel(s) and gently ease it into
shape, steaming to size, pinning
where necessary. Allow to dry
completely.

BOWTIE WRAP

DESIGNED BY LORNA MISER

KNIT/EASY

Vintage charm! This stylish wrap can be worn with everything from your favorite evening outfit to jeans and a T-shirt. The glittery yarn is spiced up with metallic organza ribbon.

SIZE

S (M, L)

Circumference 40 (45, 50)" (101.5 [114.5, 127] cm)

Length 17 (17, 20)" (43 [43, 51] cm)

Note Pattern is written for smallest size with changes for larger sizes in parentheses. When only one number is given, it applies to all sizes. To follow pattern more easily, circle all numbers pertaining to your size before beginning.

MATERIALS

 LION BRAND GLITTERSPUN 60% ACRYLIC, 13% POLYESTER, 27% CUPRO 1¾ OZ (50 G) 115 YD (105 M) BALL

4 (5, 6) balls #135 Bronze or color of your choice

- Size 10 (6 mm) knitting needles *or size to obtain gauge*

- ½ yard (0.5 m) 2½" (6.5 cm) wide organza ribbon (optional)

- Large-eyed, blunt needle

GAUGE

14 stitches + 20 rows = 4" (10 cm) in stockinette stitch (knit on right side, purl on wrong side).
Be sure to check your gauge.

WRAP

Cast on 60 (60, 70) stitches. Work even in stockinette stitch for 42 (47, 52)" (106.5 [119.5, 132] cm). (Some width is taken up when gathering the Center front.) Bind off all stitches. Sew bound-off edge to cast-on edge.

CENTER GATHERS

Using a large-eyed, blunt needle, sew a long double-strand of Glitterspun between every 3–4

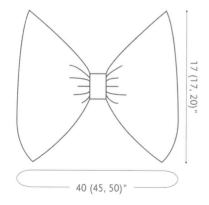

17 (17, 20)"

40 (45, 50)"

stitches up one side of seam and down the other. Pull tight to form even gathers.

BOWTIE

Cast on 20 stitches. Work even in stockinette stitch for 9" (23 cm). Bind off. Sew side edges together to form a long tube. Wrap tube around center gathers and seam ends together on inside of Wrap.

OPTIONAL RIBBON BOW

Fold ribbon in half and wrap around the Center Gathers. Pin or sew in place on inside.

BOWTIE WRAP

MESH PONCHO

DESIGNED BY DORIS CHAN

CROCHET/INTERMEDIATE

If you have a penchant for ponchos, this multihued stunner made with ribbon and a bead-trimmed fringe is a must.

SIZE

Circumference 24" (61 cm) at neck; 106" (269 cm) at lower edge
Length 23" (58.5 cm) at points

MATERIALS

 LION BRAND INCREDIBLE 100% POLYMIDE 1¾ OZ (50 G) 110 YD (100 M) BALL

6 balls #203 City Lights or color of your choice

- Size P-15 (10 mm) crochet hook *or size to obtain gauge*

- 120¼" black glass beads

- Size 14 (2.2 mm) steel crochet hook for adding beads

GAUGE

5 single crochet = 3" (7.5 cm).
1 pattern repeat = 5" (12.5 cm); 5 rows in pattern = 4" (10 cm).
Be sure to check your gauge.

STITCH EXPLANATIONS

Base chain/single crochet Start with a slip knot, chain 2, insert hook in 2nd chain from hook, draw up a loop, yarn over, draw through 1 loop, yarn over and draw through 2 loops—1 single crochet with its own chain at bottom. Work next stitch under loops of that chain. Insert hook under 2 loops at bottom of the previous stitch, draw up a loop, yarn over and draw through 1 loop, yarn over and draw through 2 loops. Repeat for length of foundation.

Slip bead On the work, drop loop from the large hook. Slip 1 bead on steel hook. Insert steel hook in dropped loop, keeping a firm hold of loop so that it doesn't enlarge. Apply some tension to loop to keep it firmly against tip of steel hook. Using your thumb, guide bead down hook and onto loop and draw through only enough loop to accommodate large hook. Reinsert large hook, continue work, and snug up next stitch to secure.

2-double crochet bobble Yarn over, insert hook into stitch and draw up loop, yarn over and draw through 2 loops. Yarn over, insert hook in same stitch and draw up a loop. Yarn over, draw through 2 loops, yarn over, draw through all loops on hook.

Bobble [Yarn over, insert hook in stitch and draw up a loop, yarn over and draw through 2 loops] 3 times in same stitch or space, yarn over, draw through all loops on hook.

PONCHO

Base chain/single crochet 40; without twisting base chain/single crochet, join with slip stitch to form ring.

Round 1 (Right Side) Chain 3, 2-double crochet bobble in first single crochet, *chain 3, skip next 2 single crochet, single crochet in each of next 5 single crochet, chain 3, skip next 2 single crochet, [bobble, chain 3, bobble] in next single crochet for corner; repeat from * 2 more times, chain 3, skip next 2 single crochet, single crochet in each of next 5 single crochet, chain 3, skip next 2 single crochet, bobble in first single crochet [already holding chain 3, 2-double crochet bobble], chain 1. Join with half double crochet in top of beginning chain [instead of last chain 3-space]. Turn—4 corner chain 3-spaces.

Round 2 Chain 1, 3 single crochet in corner space, *single crochet in next bobble, single crochet in next chain 3-space, chain 3, skip next single crochet, single crochet in each of next 3 single crochet, chain 3, single crochet in next chain 3-space, single crochet in next bobble, 5 single crochet in next corner chain 3-space; repeat from * around, ending with 2 single crochet in beginning corner space. Join with slip stitch in first single crochet.

Round 3 Chain 3, 2-double crochet bobble in first single crochet, *chain 3, single crochet in each of next 4 single crochet, single crochet in next chain 3-space, chain 3, skip next single crochet, bobble in next single crochet, chain 3, single crochet in next chain 3-space, single crochet in each of next 4 single crochet, chain 3, bobble in next single crochet; repeat from * around, omitting last bobble. Join with slip stitch in top of beginning chain—8 bobbles.

Round 4 Chain 1, single crochet in bobble, *single crochet in next chain 3-space, chain 3, skip next single crochet, single crochet in each of next 3 single crochet, chain 3, single crochet in next chain 3-space, single crochet in next bobble; repeat from * around, omitting final single crochet. Join with slip stitch in first single crochet.

Round 5 Chain 1, *single crochet in single crochet, single crochet in next single crochet, single crochet in next chain 3-space, chain 3, skip next single crochet, bobble in next single crochet, chain 3, single crochet in next chain 3-space, single crochet in next single crochet; repeat from * around. Join with slip stitch in first single crochet.

Round 6 Chain 1, *single crochet in single crochet, single crochet in next single crochet, chain 3, single crochet in next chain 3-space, single crochet in next bobble, single crochet in next chain 3-space, chain 3, skip next single crochet, single crochet in next single crochet; repeat from * around. Join with slip stitch in first single crochet.

Round 7 Chain 3, 2-double crochet bobble in first single crochet, *chain 3, single crochet in next chain 3-space, single crochet in each of next 3 single crochet, single crochet in next chain 3-space, chain 3, skip next single crochet, bobble in next single crochet, chain 3, single crochet in next chain 3-space, single crochet in each of next 3 single crochet, chain 3, skip next single crochet, [bobble, chain 3, bobble] in next single crochet for corner increase; repeat from * around, ending with bobble in beginning space, chain 1. Join with half double crochet in top of beginning chain—12 bobbles.

Round 8 Chain 1, 3 single crochet in corner space, *single crochet in next bobble, single crochet in next chain 3-space, chain 3, skip next single crochet, single crochet in each of next 3 single crochet, chain 3, single crochet in next chain 3-space, single crochet in next bobble, single crochet in next chain 3-space, chain 3, skip next single crochet, single crochet in each of next 3 single crochet, chain 3, single crochet in next chain 3-space, single crochet in next bobble, 5 single crochet in next corner chain 3-space; repeat from * around, ending with 2 single crochet in beginning space. Join with slip stitch in first single crochet.

Round 9 Chain 3, 2-double crochet bobble in first single crochet, *chain 3, single crochet in each of next 4 single crochet, single crochet in next chain 3-space, chain 3, skip next single crochet, bobble in next single crochet, chain 3, single crochet in next chain 3-space,

single crochet in each of next 3 single crochet, single crochet in next chain 3-space, chain 3, skip next single crochet, bobble in next single crochet, chain 3, single crochet in next chain 3-space, single crochet in each of next 4 single crochet, chain 3, bobble in next single crochet; repeat from * around, omitting last bobble; join with slip stitch in top of beginning chain—12 bobbles.

Rounds 10–15 Repeat Rounds 4–9, maintaining established increase pattern—16 bobbles at end of Round 15.

Rounds 16–21 Repeat Rounds 4–9, maintaining established increase pattern—20 bobbles at end of Round 21.

Round 22 Repeat Round 4.

Round 23 *[chain 11, slip bead,

chain 1, slip stitch in each last 11 chain, slip stitch in same single crochet] twice, chain 5, skip next 2 single crochet, bobble in next single crochet (center of 3–single crochet group), chain 5, skip next 2 single crochet, slip stitch in next single crochet (center of 3–single crochet group); repeat from * around—20 sets of double-tails; 40 beaded ends. Fasten off.

NECK EDGING

With right side facing, join yarn in any single crochet on opposite side of base chain/single crochet, chain 1, single crochet in each single crochet around. Join with slip stitch in first single crochet—40 single crochet. Fasten off. Weave in ends.

6.

WRAPS PLUS

In this chapter we use deceptively simple construction as a point of departure. The Kimono Shrug is a modern appropriation of non-Western construction. The drape of the Silky Swathe belies the geometry of the garment. It is nothing more than a large rectangle knitted with two armhole slits. When worn, it falls asymmetrically from the shoulders. Shrug My Shoulders is another simple shape transformed by the addition of contrasting ties. The simplicity of these wraps makes them wonderful candidates for embellishing with vintage pin closures and brooches. The ties on both Shrug My Shoulders and the Kimono Shrug can be adapted to include buckle closures or brooch closures. All these garments are proof that less is more.

KIMONO SHRUG

DESIGNED BY VLADIMIR TERIOKHIN

KNIT/EASY

If there's anything better than a stylish easy knit, it's a stylish easy knit you can wear in a variety of ways. This exotic shrug can be worn with the ties at your neck or at your waist.

SIZE

Width 44" (112 cm) cuff-to-cuff
Length 15" (38 cm)

MATERIALS

LION BRAND MICROSPUN
100% MICROFIBER ACRYLIC
2½ OZ (70 G) 168 YD (154 M)
BALL

8 balls #113 Cherry Red or color of your choice

• Size 4 (3.5 mm) 24" (61 cm) circular needle *or size to obtain gauge*

• Stitch marker

• Large-eyed, blunt needle

GAUGE

24 stitches + 32 rounds = 4" (10 cm) in stockinette stitch (knit every round).
Be sure to check your gauge.

SLEEVES

Cast on 204 stitches. Place marker and join for working in the round, being careful not to twist.
Work even in stockinette stitch until piece measures 17" (43 cm). Bind off all stitches.

BACK

Cast on 84 stitches. Working in stockinette stitch (knit on right side, purl on wrong side), decrease 1 stitch each end of row every 10th row 12 times—60 stitches. Bind off.

TIE

Cast on 20 stitches.
Row 1 Purl 2, [knit 1, purl 1] 8 times, knit 2.
Repeat Row 1 until piece measures 84" (213.5 cm). Bind off all stitches in pattern.

FINISHING

Lay Sleeves flat with right side out. With right side facing, place side edge of Back against top edge of Sleeve and sew across half of Sleeve opening. Repeat for other side. Mark center 14" (35.5 cm) of Tie. Sew to lower edge of Back. Weave in ends.

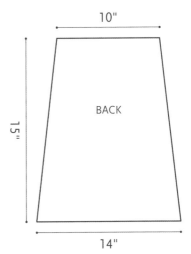

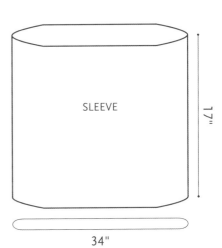

TIE

2"

84"

SLEEVE

17"

34"

10"

BACK

15"

14"

SHRUG MY SHOULDERS

DESIGNED BY DIANA RUPP

KNIT/EASY

This wrap is casual dressing at its most sophisticated. The contrasting waist ties transform the deceptively simple rectangular garment.

SIZE

Finished Chest 32" (81.5 cm)
(Bolero does not close at front)
Length 14" (35.5 cm)

MATERIALS

 LION BRAND MOONLIGHT MOHAIR
35% MOHAIR, 30% ACRYLIC, 25% COTTON, 10% METALLIC POLYESTER
1¾ OZ (50 G) 82 YD (75 M) BALL

2 balls #205 Glacier Bay (A) or color of your choice

 LION BRAND WOOL-EASE
80% ACRYLIC, 20% WOOL
3 OZ (85 G) 197 YD (180 M) BALL

1 ball #170 Peacock (B) or color of your choice

• Size 13 (9 mm) knitting needles
  or size to obtain gauge

- Size 8 (5 mm) knitting needles *or size to obtain gauge*

- Large-eyed, blunt needle

GAUGE

12 stitches + 12 rows = 4" (10 cm) in garter stitch (knit every row) with A on larger needles.
17 stitches + 22 rows = 4" (10 cm) in Knit 1, Purl 1 rib with B on smaller needles.
Be sure to check your gauge.

BODY PANEL (MAKE 2)

With larger needles and A, cast on 24 stitches. Work in garter stitch until piece measures 28" (71 cm) from beginning. Bind off.

BELT

With smaller needles and B, cast on 16 stitches. Work in knit 1, purl 1 rib until piece measures 48" (122 cm) from beginning. Bind off.

FINISHING

Lay Body Panels next to each other with long sides together. Sew center seam from bottom for 13" (33 cm). Fold Panels in half, bringing top edge down to meet bottom edge. Whipstitch side seams from bottom for 7½" (19 cm), leaving openings for arms. Whipstitch Belt to lower edge of Body Panels, matching every other garter stitch on Body to each stitch on Belt. (Waist will gather.) Weave in ends.

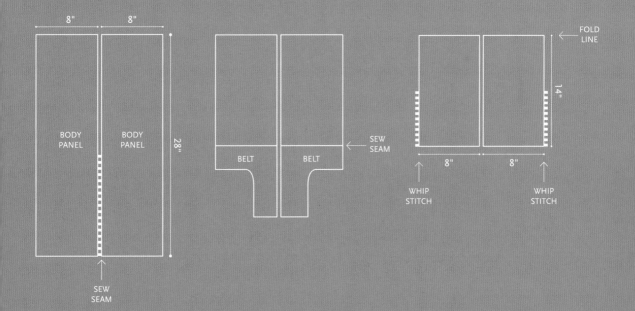

SILKY SWATHE

DESIGNED BY CATHY MAGUIRE

KNIT/EASY

This rectangular wrap is made with two openings for the arms. It drapes beautifully and can be worn in a host of stylish ways: cross in front and secure with a brooch as shown, let the ends hang loose, or throw one side over your shoulder.

SIZE

Circumference 60" (152.5 cm)
Length 30" (76 cm)

MATERIALS

 LION BRAND MICROSPUN
100% MICROFIBER ACRYLIC
2½ OZ (70 G) 168 YD (154 M)
BALL

10 balls #149 Silver Grey or color of your choice

- Size 7 (4.5 mm) knitting needles
  or size to obtain gauge

- 2 small kilt pins

GAUGE

20 stitches + 28 rows = 4" (10 cm) in stockinette stitch (knit on right side, purl on wrong side).
Be sure to check your gauge.

PATTERN STITCHES

Seed stitch (multiple of 2 stitches + 1)

Row 1 *Knit 1, purl 1; repeat from *, ending knit 1.
Repeat Row 1 for seed stitch.
Seed stitch (multiple of 2 stitches)
Row 1 (Right Side) *Knit 1, purl 1; repeat from * across.
Row 2 *Purl 1, knit 1; repeat from * across.
Repeat Rows 1–2 for seed stitch.

NOTE

Wrap is knit vertically in one piece starting at right center front, working to back, then continuing to left center front.

WRAP

Cast on 133 stitches.
Rows 1–4 Work in seed stitch.
Rows 5–144 Work first 3 stitches in seed stitch, work center 127 stitches in stockinette stitch, work last 3 stitches in seed stitch.

ARMHOLE BORDER

Row 145 Work 3 stitches in seed stitch, 20 stitches in stockinette stitch, 44 stitches in seed stitch, 63 stitches in stockinette stitch, 3 stitches in seed stitch.

Row 146 Work 3 stitches in seed stitch, 63 stitches in stockinette stitch, 44 stitches in seed stitch, 20 stitches in stockinette stitch, 3 stitches in seed stitch.

ARMHOLE OPENING

Row 147 Work 3 stitches in seed stitch, 20 stitches in stockinette stitch, 3 stitches in seed stitch, bind off next 39 stitches in pattern, 2 stitches in seed stitch, 63 stitches in stockinette stitch, 3 stitches in seed stitch—26 stitches at start of row, 68 stitches at end of row.
Row 148 Work 3 stitches in seed stitch, 63 stitches in stockinette

stitch, 2 stitches in seed stitch, cast on 39 stitches, 3 stitches in seed stitch, 20 stitches in stockinette stitch, 3 stitches in seed stitch— 133 stitches.

ARMHOLE BORDER

Rows 149–150 Repeat Rows 145–146.

Rows 151–272 Work first 3 stitches in seed stitch, work center 127 stitches in stockinette stitch, work last 3 stitches in seed stitch.

ARMHOLE

Rows 273–278 Repeat Rows 145–150.

Rows 279–418 Work first 3 stitches in seed stitch, work center 127 stitches in stockinette stitch, work last 3 stitches in seed stitch.

Rows 419–422 Work in seed stitch. Bind off all stitches.

FINISHING

Weave in all ends. Steam lightly to shape.

SILKY SWATHE

7.
ALL WRAPPED UP

This chapter weaves all your new skills together. When you've mastered crochet, you can go wild with a freeform sculpted stole or create a vintage-inspired capelet. If you can knit and embroider, Little Red is a great way of showing off your skills. The Technicolor Cape is a beautifully shaped classic with snap closures and a chance to fuel your creativity with color and texture.

LITTLE RED

DESIGNED BY GALINA CARROLL

KNIT WITH EMBROIDERY/INTERMEDIATE

This chic little poncho will be loved by tots and tweens alike. The chain stitch embroidery in contrasting colors is a fun and easy finish.

SIZE

Circumference 18" (45.5 cm) at neck; 57" (145 cm) at lower edge

MATERIALS

 LION BRAND WOOL-EASE
80% ACRYLIC, 20% WOOL
3 OZ (85 G) 197 YD (180 M) BALL

4 balls #102 Ranch Red or color of your choice

- Size 8 (5 mm) 29" (74 cm) circular needle *or size to obtain gauge*

- Stitch markers

- Large-eyed, blunt needle

- Embroidery floss and needle (optional)

GAUGE

16 stitches + 22 rounds = 4" (10 cm) in stockinette stitch (knit every round).
Be sure to check your gauge.

STITCH EXPLANATIONS

Wrap and turn Bring yarn forward, slip 1 stitch as if to purl, yarn back, transfer slipped stitch back onto left needle, turn work.

Ssk (slip, slip, knit) Slip next 2 stitches one at a time, to right needle, as if to knit; insert left needle into fronts of these 2 stitches and knit them together.

HEM

Cast on 228 stitches. Place marker for beginning of round and join, being careful not to twist.
Rounds 1–5 Knit.
Round 6 Purl. (This will be the turning round for the hem.)
Rounds 7–11 Knit.

PONCHO FRONT

Round 12 (Set-up Round) Knit 24, place marker, knit 3 together, knit 60, knit 3 together, place marker, knit 24, place marker (for side), knit 24, place marker, knit 3 together, knit 60, knit 3 together, place marker, knit 24—220 stitches.

Round 13 Knit to 2nd marker, remove marker, knit 1. Wrap and turn.

Continue working back and forth in short rows as follows:

Row 1 Purl to next marker, remove marker, purl 1. Wrap and turn.

Row 2 Knit to 1 stitch past wrap from previous knit row. Wrap and turn.

Row 3 Purl to 1 stitch past wrap from previous purl row. Wrap and turn.

Repeat Rows 2–3 until all Poncho Front stitches are worked. (Work up to side and beginning of round markers.)

PONCHO BACK

Knit across front stitches to side marker. Continue as for Poncho Front, beginning with Round 13. After shaping is complete, knit to beginning of round.

SHAPE SIDES

Continue working in the round.

Round 1 [Knit 1, ssk, knit to 3 stitches before marker, knit 2 together, knit 1] 2 times.

Round 2 Knit.

Repeat Rounds 1–2 until the center front measures 15" (38 cm).

FRONT PLACKET

Note Poncho is now worked back and forth in rows.

Mark center of front.

Row 1 Knit 1, ssk, knit to center of front, purl 3, knit to 3 stitches before marker, knit 2 together, knit 1, slip marker, knit 1, ssk, knit to 3 stitches before marker, knit 2 together, knit 1, slip beginning of round marker, knit to 3 stitches before center front, purl 3. Turn.

Row 2 (Wrong Side) Purl.

Row 3 (Right Side) Purl 3, knit to 3 stitches before marker, knit 2 together, knit 1, slip marker, knit 1, ssk, knit to 3 stitches before marker, knit 2 together, knit 1, slip beginning of round marker, knit to last 3 stitches, purl 3.

Repeat Rows 2–3 until 120 stitches remain, ending with a wrong side row.

SHAPE SHOULDER

Next Row (Right Side) Purl 3, knit 9, [knit 2 together] 9 times, slip marker, [knit 2 together] 3 times, knit 2, knit 2 together, [knit 4, knit 2 together] 7 times, knit 2, [knit 2 together] 3 times, slip marker, [knit 2 together] 9 times, knit 9, purl 3—88 stitches.

Next Row Purl.

Next Row Purl 3, knit 12, [knit 2 together] 3 times, slip marker, [knit 1, knit 2 together] twice, [knit 3, knit 2 together] 3 times, knit 4, [knit 2 together, knit 3] 3 times, [knit 2 together, knit 1] twice, slip marker, [knit 2 together] 3 times, knit 12, purl 3—72 stitches.

Next Row Purl.

SHAPE BACK NECK

Row 1 (Right Side) Purl 3, knit to first marker, knit 30. Wrap and turn.

Row 2 (Wrong Side) Purl 24. Wrap and turn.

Row 3 Knit 23. Wrap and turn.

Row 4 Purl 22. Wrap and turn.

Row 5 Knit 21. Wrap and turn.

Row 6 Purl 20. Wrap and turn.

Row 7 Knit 19. Wrap and turn.

Row 8 Purl 18. Wrap and turn.

Row 9 Knit to last 3 stitches, purl 3.

SCARF

Without turning, cast on 42 stitches. Turn. Purl next row, then cast on 42 stitches. Continue in stockinette stitch (knit on right side, purl on wrong side) until Scarf measures 3" (7.5 cm). Bind off.

FINISHING

Sew hem. Weave in ends.

OPTIONAL

If desired, use 2 strands of embroidery floss in a variety of colors and chain stitch spirals randomly across Poncho, as shown.

TECHNICOLOR CAPE

DESIGNED BY VLADIMIR TERIOKHIN

KNIT/INTERMEDIATE

This straightforward take on the cape closes with jumbo snaps and features flattering shoulder shaping and useful hand slits.

SIZE
Width 30" (76 cm) at lower edge
Length 26½" (67.5 cm)

MATERIALS

 LION BRAND LANDSCAPES
50% WOOL, 50% ACRYLIC
1¾ OZ (50 G) 55 YD (50 M) BALL

10 balls #276 Summer Fields or color of your choice

- Size 10.5 (6.5 mm) knitting needles *or size to obtain gauge*

- Stitch holders

- 3 sets ⅞" (22 mm) metal snaps

- Large-eyed, blunt needle

GAUGE
11 stitches + 15 rows = 4" (10 cm) in stockinette stitch (knit on right side, purl on wrong side).
Be sure to check your gauge.

STITCH EXPLANATION
Ssk (slip, slip, knit) Slip next 2 stitches as if to knit, one at a time, to right needle; insert left needle into fronts of these 2 stitches and knit them together.

BACK
Cast on 82 stitches. Knit 3 rows. Change to stockinette stitch and work even until piece measures 14" (35.5 cm) from beginning, ending with a wrong side row.

SHAPE BODY
Decrease Row Knit 2, ssk, knit to last 4 stitches, knit 2 together, knit 2.
Work Decrease Row every other row 20 times total—42 stitches.
Shape Shoulder (Right Side) Bind off 3 stitches at beginning of next row, knit 10—11 stitches for right shoulder. Join 2nd ball of yarn, bind off 14 stitches, work to end of row.

Bind off 2 stitches at each neck edge once. At the same time, working both sides at once, bind off 3 stitches at beginning of next 7 rows.

RIGHT FRONT
Cast on 44 stitches. Knit 3 rows.
Next Row (Right Side) Knit.
Next Row (Wrong Side) Purl 40, knit 4.
Repeat last 2 rows until piece measures 5" (12.5 cm) from beginning, ending with a right side row.

HAND OPENING
Left Side Purl 20, knit 4; place remaining stitches on holder for right side. Continue even on 24 stitches, keeping 4 edge stitches in garter stitch (knit every row), for 25 rows total, ending with a wrong side row. Break yarn. Place stitches on holder.
Right Side With wrong side facing,

pick up and knit 4 stitches behind base of garter stitch edge of Left Side; place stitches from holder onto needle, purl 16, knit 4—24 stitches. Work even, keeping first and last 4 edge stitches in garter stitch, for 25 rows total, ending with a wrong side row.

JOIN SIDES

Place stitches from holder onto separate needle. Knit 20 from Right Side; placing Left Side behind Right Side, *knit next stitch from Right Side together with first/next stitch from Left Side; repeat from * 3 more times, knit to end of row—44 stitches.

Continue even in stockinette stitch, keeping 4 front edge stitches in garter stitch, until piece measures 14" (35.5 cm) from beg, ending with a wrong side row.

SHAPE BODY

Decrease Row Knit to last 4 stitches, knit 2 together, knit 2. Repeat Decrease Row every other row 20 times total—24 stitches. **Shape Neck and Shoulder (Right Side)** Bind off 6 stitches, knit to end of row. [Bind off 3 stitches, purl to end of row; bind off 2

stitches, knit to end of row] 3 times. Bind off remaining 3 stitches.

LEFT FRONT

Work as for Right Front, reversing shaping.

FINISHING

Sew Shoulder, Body, and Side seams.

COLLAR

Pick up and knit 50 stitches evenly spaced around neck opening, including garter edges. Knit 20 rows in garter stitch. Bind off all stitches. Weave in ends. Sew snaps ½" (13 mm), 3½" (9 cm), and 6½" (16.5 cm) from top edges of Collar (measured at center of snaps).

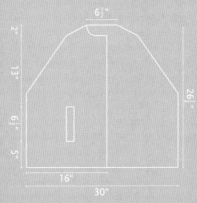

FUR-TRIMMED PONCHO

DESIGNED BY
VLADIMIR TERIOKHIN

KNIT/INTERMEDIATE

This elegant poncho is shaped for a perfect fit. The suede-looking and faux fur yarns make a guilt-free fashion statement.

SIZE

Circumference 17½" (44.5 cm) at neck; 83" (211 cm) at lower edge
Length 24" (61 cm)

MATERIALS

 LION BRAND LION SUEDE
100% POLYESTER
3 OZ (85 G) 122 YD (110 M) BALL

10 balls #125 Mocha (main color) or color of your choice

 LION BRAND FUN FUR
100% POLYESTER
1¾ OZ (20 G) 64 YD (58 M) BALL

6 balls #126 Chocolate (contrasting color) or color of your choice

• Size 6 (4 mm) 16" (40.5 cm) and
  24" (61 cm) circular needles
  or size to obtain gauge

- Stitch markers (3 different colors—A, B, and C)

GAUGE

11 stitches + 24 rounds = 4" (10 cm) in stockinette stitch (knit every round) with main color.
Be sure to check your gauge.

PONCHO

With 2 strands of contrasting color held together and shorter needle, cast on 48 stitches. Place marker A and join for working in the round. Work in garter stitch (purl 1 round, knit 1 round) for 6" (15 cm). Cut contrasting color and join main color. Knit 4, place marker C; knit 5, place marker B; knit 6, place marker B; knit 5, place marker C; knit 8, place marker C; knit 5, place marker B; knit 6, place marker B; knit 5, place marker C; knit 4.

Note Increases are made in stitches just outside of marked stitches (center stitches marked by C markers and shoulder stitches marked by B markers). Center and shoulder increases are worked at the same time, but at different rates. Change to longer needle when necessary.

Center Increase Round *Knit to next marker C, knit into front and back of next stitch, knit to 1 stitch before next marker C, knit into back and front of next stitch; repeat from * once more, knit to end of round. Repeat Center Increase Round every 4th round 25 times total. At the same time, work shoulder increases.

Shoulder Increase Round *K to 1 stitch before next marker B, knit into back and front of next stitch, knit to next marker B, knit into front and back of next stitch; repeat from * once more, knit to end of round. Repeat Shoulder Increase Round every 2nd round 10 times total; every 6th round 7 times; then every 12th round 3 times. Work 2 rounds even.

When all increases have been made, cut main color—228 stitches. Join 2 strands of contrasting color and work in garter stitch for 3" (7.5 cm). Bind off all stitches. Weave in ends.

CONEY ISLAND CAPELET

DESIGNED BY VLADIMIR TERIOKHIN

CROCHET/EASY

Fur trim adds a touch of elegance to this simple shaped capelet—perfect for an evening stroll on the boardwalk.

SIZE
One size fits most
Circumference 27" (68.5 cm) neckband
Length 13" (33 cm)

MATERIALS

 LION BRAND HOMESPUN
98% ACRYLIC, 2% POLYESTER
6 OZ (170 G) 185 YD (167 M)
SKEINS

3 skeins #343 Romanesque or color of your choice

 LION BRAND FUN FUR
100% POLYESTER SOLID COLORS:
1¾ OZ (50 G) 64 YD (58 M) BALLS
PRINTS: 1½ OZ (40 G) 57 YD (52 M) BALLS

1 ball #204 Lava print or color of your choice

• Size K-10.5 (6.5 mm) crochet hook *or size to obtain gauge*

GAUGE
12 double crochet + 7 rows = 4" (10 cm) using Homespun.
Be sure to check your gauge.

NOTE
Neckband is worked first, then body of Cape and Collar are worked from the Neckband down.

NECKBAND
With Homespun, chain 5.
Row 1 Single crochet in 2nd chain from hook and in each chain across. Turn—4 single crochet.
Row 2 Chain 3 (counts as 1 double crochet), double crochet in next 3 stitches. Turn.
Repeat this row until Neckband measures 27" (68.5 cm). Turn.
Next row Chain 1, single crochet in each of next 3 double crochet, single crochet in top of beginning chain-3; rotate to side, work 84 single crochet evenly spaced along side edge to end. Turn.

CAPE
Row 1 Chain 3, double crochet in each of next 6 stitches, *2 double crochet in next stitch, double crochet in each of next 6 stitches; repeat from * to end. Turn—95 double crochet.
Row 2 Work 1 row even in double crochet. Turn.
Row 3 Chain 3, double crochet in next stitch, *2 double crochet in next stitch, double crochet in each of next 6 stitches; repeat from * to last 2 stitches, 2 double crochet in next stitch, double crochet in last stitch. Turn—109 double crochet.
Rows 4–7 Work 4 rows even in double crochet. Turn.
Row 8 Chain 3, double crochet in next stitch, *2 double crochet in next stitch, double crochet in next 6

stitches; repeat from * to last 2
stitches; 2 double crochet in next
stitch, double crochet in last stitch.
Turn—125 double crochet.

Rows 9–11 Work 3 rows even in
double crochet. Turn.

Row 12 Chain 3, double crochet in
next 2 stitches, *2 double crochet
in next stitch, double crochet in
next 6 stitches; repeat from * to
last 3 stitches, 2 double crochet in
next stitch, double crochet in last 2
stitches. Turn—143 double crochet.

Rows 13–16 Work 4 rows even in
double crochet. Turn.

Row 17 Chain 3, double crochet in
next 7 stitches, *2 double crochet
in next stitch, double crochet in
next 8 stitches; repeat from *
across. Turn—158 double crochet.

Rows 18–19 Work 2 rows even in
double crochet. Fasten off. Sew
ends of Neckband together.

COLLAR

Note Collar is worked back and
forth in rows.

Row 1 With right side facing,
Neckband at bottom, and working
along single crochet row (the first
row that Cape is worked into) and
on top of Cape, join Homespun
with a slip stitch at seam. Chain 3,

double crochet in next 4 stitches, *2 double crochet in next stitch, double crochet in next 5 stitches; repeat from * to last stitch, double crochet in last stitch. Turn—97 stitches.

Row 2 Chain 3, double crochet in next stitch, 2 double crochet in next stitch, double crochet in next 6 stitches; repeat from * to last 4 stitches, 2 double crochet in next stitch, double crochet in last 3 stitches. Turn—111 stitches.

Row 3 Work 1 row even in double crochet. Turn.

Row 4 Chain 3, double crochet in next 4 stitches, 2 double crochet in next stitch, *double crochet in next 8 stitches, 2 double crochet in next st; repeat from * to last 6 stitches, double crochet in last 6 stitches. Turn—123 stitches.

Row 5 Chain 3, double crochet in next 11 stitches, 2 double crochet in next stitch, *double crochet in next 10 stitches, 2 double crochet in next st; repeat from * to last 11 stitches, double crochet in last 11 stitches. Turn—133 stitches. Fasten off Homespun.

Row 6 With 2 strands of Fun Fur held together, join with a slip stitch in first stitch, chain 1, single crochet in first stitch and in each double crochet across.

Row 7 Chain 1, single crochet in each single crochet across. Turn.

Row 8 Chain 1, single crochet in first stitch and next 7 stitches, 2 single crochet in next stitch, *single crochet in next 12 stitches, 2 single crochet in next st; repeat from * to last 7 stitches, single crochet in last 7 stitches—143 stitches. Do not turn.

COLLAR EDGING

Rotate to side, work 2 single crochet in corner, then 1 single crochet in each single crochet row and 2 single crochet in each double crochet row to first row of Collar. Repeat along other edge of Collar to corner. Join with a slip stitch. Fasten off.

CAPE EDGING

With Homespun and right side facing, join in left side corner of Cape with a slip stitch. Chain 1, work 1 single crochet in each double crochet around to right side corner, 3 single crochet in corner. Working along Cape edge, work 2 single crochet in each double crochet row to first row, then repeat along other edge to corner. Work 3 single crochet in corner. Join with a slip stitch. Fasten off.

NECKBAND EDGING

Join Homespun with a slip stitch in any stitch along top of Neckband edge. Chain 1, work 84 single crochet evenly spaced around. Join with a slip stitch.
Fasten off. Weave in ends.

SCULPTED STOLE

DESIGNED BY SHEILA PEPE

CROCHET/EXPERIENCED

This wrap showcases the unique design skills and color sensibilities of noted crochet artist and sculptor Sheila Pepe. Sculptural and experimental, this project combines interesting colors, textures, and shapes.

SIZE

40" wide x 20" deep (101.5 x 51 cm), plus fringe

MATERIALS

 LION BRAND WOOL-EASE CHUNKY 80% ACRYLIC, 20% WOOL 5 OZ (140 G) 153 YD (140 M) BALL

1 ball each #133 Pumpkin (A), #135 Spice (B), #127 Walnut (C), or colors of your choice

 LION BRAND FUN FUR 100% POLYESTER SOLID COLORS: 1³/₄ OZ (50 G) 64 YD (54 M) BALLS

1 ball #126 Chocolate (D) or color of your choice

- Size J-10 (6 mm) crochet hook *or size to obtain gauge*

- Size I-9 (5.5 mm) crochet hook *or size to obtain gauge*

- Size G-6 (4 mm) crochet hook

- Scraps of contrasting yarn to be used as markers

- Large-eyed, blunt needle

GAUGE

First 3 rounds of Circle 1 = 2" (5 cm) across on middle-sized hook. 10 single crochet = 4" (10 cm) with B on largest hook.
Be sure to check your gauge.

STITCH EXPLANATION

Single crochet 2 together (single crochet decrease) Insert hook into stitch and draw up a loop. Insert hook into next stitch and draw up a loop. Yarn over, draw through all 3 loops on hook.

NOTE

This is a "free form" design composed of 3 circle motifs and 2 oval motifs. The motifs are then connected with fillers to form an irregular rectangular shape to which edgings and fringe pieces are added. Directions are given for the motifs, but the fillers are worked in a nonspecific manner, working stitches to fill areas between the motifs.

BOTTOM HALF

CIRCLE 1

With middle-sized hook and A, chain 2.

Round 1 (Right Side) Work 6 single crochet in 2nd chain from hook. Do not join. Work in a spiral, marking beginning of each round, moving marker up as work progresses— 6 single crochet.

Round 2 [Single crochet, chain 1] in each single crochet around—6 chain 1-spaces.

Round 3 [Single crochet, chain 1, single crochet, chain 1] in each single crochet around—12 chain 1-spaces.

Round 4 *[Single crochet, chain 1] in each of next 3 chain 1-spaces, [single crochet, chain 1, single crochet, chain 1] in next chain 1-space; repeat from * around—15 chain 1-spaces.

Round 5 *[Single crochet, chain 1] in next chain 1-space, [single crochet, chain 1, single crochet, chain 1] in next chain 1-space, [single crochet, chain 1] in next chain 1-space; repeat from * around—20 chain 1-spaces.

Round 6 *[Single crochet, chain 1] in each of next 3 chain 1-spaces, [single crochet, chain 1, single crochet, chain 1] in next chain 1-space, [single crochet, chain 1] in next chain 1-space; repeat from * around—24 chain 1-spaces.

Round 7 *[Single crochet, chain 1] in each of next 5 chain 1-spaces, [single crochet, chain 1, single crochet, chain 1] in next chain 1-space; repeat from * around. Join with slip stitch in next single crochet—28 chain 1-spaces.

Round 8 *[Single crochet, chain 1] in each of next 2 chain 1-spaces, [single crochet, chain 1, single crochet, chain 1] in next chain 1-space, [single crochet, chain 1] in next chain 1-space; repeat from * around. Join with slip stitch in next single crochet—35 chain 1-spaces. Fasten off A.

Round 9 With right side facing and smallest hook, join D in any chain 1-space, chain 1, [single crochet, chain 1] in each chain 1-space around. Join with slip stitch in first single crochet—35 chain 1-spaces.

Round 10 Chain 4, [double crochet, chain 1] in same chain 1-space, [double crochet, chain 1] in each chain 1-space around. Join with slip stitch in 3rd chain of beginning chain—36 chain 1-spaces. Fasten off D.

Round 11 With right side facing and largest hook, join B in any chain 1-space, chain 1, *single crochet in each of next 2 chain 1-spaces, 2 single crochet in next chain 1-space; repeat from * around. Join with slip stitch in first single crochet—48 single crochet. Fasten off B.

LARGE OVAL

With middle-sized hook and A, chain 54.

Round 1 (Right Side) Single crochet in 2nd chain from hook and in each of next 51 chain, 3 single crochet in last chain; working across opposite side of foundation chain, single crochet in each of next 51 chain, 2 single crochet in last chain already holding 1 single crochet. Join with slip stitch in first single crochet—108 single crochet.

Round 2 Chain 1, 2 single crochet in first single crochet, single crochet in next 51 single crochet, 2 single crochet in each of next 3 single crochet, single crochet in each of next 51 single crochet, 2 single crochet in each of last 2 single crochet. Join with slip stitch in first single crochet—114 single crochet.

Round 3 Chain 1, single crochet in first single crochet, 2 single crochet in next single crochet, single crochet in each of next 51 single crochet, [single crochet in next single crochet, 2 single crochet in next single crochet] 3 times, single crochet in each of next 51 single crochet, [single crochet in next single crochet, 2 single crochet in next single crochet] twice. Join with slip stitch in first single crochet—120 single crochet.

Round 4 Chain 1, single crochet in first 2 single crochet, 2 single crochet in next single crochet, single crochet in each of next 51 single crochet, [single crochet in next 2 single crochet, 2 single crochet in next single crochet] 3 times, single crochet in each of next 51 single crochet, [single crochet in next 2 single crochet, 2 single crochet in next single crochet] twice. Join with slip stitch in first single crochet—126 single crochet. Fasten off A.

Round 5 With right side facing and smallest hook, join D in any single crochet, chain 1, single crochet in each single crochet around. Join with slip stitch in first single crochet.

Round 6 Chain 4, [double crochet, chain 1] in each of next 2 single crochet, [double crochet, chain 1, double crochet, chain 1] in next single crochet, [double crochet, chain 1] in each of next 51 single crochet, *[double crochet, chain 1] in each of next 3 single crochet, [double crochet, chain 1, double crochet, chain 1] in next single crochet *; repeat from * to * 2 more times, [double crochet, chain 1] in each of next 51 single crochet, repeat from * to * twice. Join with slip stitch in 3rd chain of beginning chain 4—132 double crochet. Fasten off D.

Round 7 With right side facing and largest hook, join B in any chain 1-space, chain 1, single crochet in each chain 1-space around. Join with slip stitch in first single crochet—132 single crochet. Fasten off.

Joining Chain With right side facing and largest hook, join B in center single crochet on one end of Large Oval, chain 9; join with slip stitch in any single crochet in last round of Circle 1.

Round 1 Chain 1, single crochet evenly spaced around Circle 1, increase as necessary to keep work flat, single crochet in each chain across Joining Chain, single crochet evenly spaced around Large Oval, single crochet in each chain across opposite side of Joining Chain. Join with slip stitch in first single crochet.

Rounds 2–3 Chain 1, single crochet evenly spaced around, increase around curved ends and decrease (by working single crochet 2 together) at inner corners as necessary to keep work flat. Join with slip stitch in first single crochet. Fasten off B.

Round 4 With right side facing, join C in first single crochet, chain 1, single crochet evenly spaced

around, increase around curved ends and decrease at inner corners as necessary to keep work flat. Join with slip stitch in first single crochet. Fasten off.

TOP HALF
CIRCLE 2

Work as for Circle 1 through Round 11. Do not fasten off at end of Round 11.

Round 12 Chain 1, *single crochet in each of next 5 single crochet, 2 single crochet in next single crochet; repeat from * around. Join with slip stitch in first single crochet—56 single crochet. Fasten off B.

Round 13 With right side facing, join C in any single crochet, chain 1, *single crochet in each of next 11 single crochet, 2 single crochet in next single crochet; repeat from * around, ending with single crochet in each of next 7 single crochet, 2 single crochet in last single crochet. Join with slip stitch in first single crochet—61 single crochet. Fasten off.

CIRCLE 3

Work as for Circle 2 through Round 12. Do not fasten off.

Round 13 With B, chain 1, *single

crochet in each of next 11 single crochet, 2 single crochet in next single crochet; repeat from * around, ending with single crochet in each of next 7 single crochet, 2 single crochet in last single crochet. Join with slip stitch in first single crochet—61 single crochet. Fasten off B.

Round 14 With right side facing, join C in any single crochet, chain 1, *single crochet in each of next 4 single crochet, 2 single crochet in next single crochet; repeat from * around, ending with single crochet in last single crochet. Join with slip stitch in first single crochet—73 single crochet. Fasten off.

SMALL OVAL

With middle-sized hook and A, chain 32.

Round 1 (Right Side) Single crochet in 2nd chain from hook and in each of next 29 chains, 3 single crochet in last chain; working across opposite side of foundation chain, single crochet in each of next 29 chain, 2 single crochet in last chain already holding 1 single crochet. Join with slip stitch in first single crochet—64 single crochet.

Round 2 Chain 1, 2 single crochet

in first single crochet, single crochet in next 29 single crochet, 2 single crochet in each of next 3 single crochet, single crochet in each of next 29 single crochet, 2 single crochet in each of last 2 single crochet. Join with slip stitch in first single crochet—70 single crochet.

Round 3 Chain 1, single crochet in first single crochet, 2 single crochet in next single crochet, single crochet in each of next 29 single crochet, [single crochet in next single crochet, 2 single crochet in next single crochet] 3 times, single crochet in each of next 29 single crochet, [single crochet in next single crochet, 2 single crochet in next single crochet] twice. Join with slip stitch in first single crochet—76 single crochet.

Round 4 Chain 1, single crochet in first 2 single crochet, 2 single crochet in next single crochet, single crochet in each of next 29 single crochet, [single crochet in next 2 single crochet, 2 single crochet in next single crochet] 3 times, single crochet in each of next 29 single crochet, [single crochet in next 2 single crochet, 2 single crochet in next single crochet] twice. Join with slip stitch in first single crochet—

82 single crochet. Fasten off A.

Round 5 With right side facing and smallest hook, join D in any single crochet, chain 1, single crochet in each single crochet around. Join with slip stitch in first single crochet.

Round 6 Chain 4, [double crochet, chain 1] in each of next 2 single crochet, [double crochet, chain 1, double crochet, chain 1] in next single crochet, [double crochet, chain 1] in each of next 29 single crochet, *[double crochet, chain 1] in each of next 3 single crochet, [double crochet, chain 1, double crochet, chain 1] in next single crochet *; repeat from * to * 2 more times, [double crochet, chain 1] in each of next 29 single crochet, repeat from * to * twice. Join with slip stitch in 3rd chain of beginning chain 4—88 chain 1-spaces. Fasten off D.

Round 7 With right side facing and largest hook, join B in any chain 1-space, chain 1, single crochet in each chain 1-space around, working 4 increases evenly spaced around each end of Oval. Join with slip stitch in first single crochet—96 single crochet.

Round 8 Chain 1, single crochet in each single crochet around, working 4 increases evenly spaced

around each end of Oval. Join with slip stitch in first single crochet—104 single crochet.

Round 9 Chain 1, single crochet in each single crochet around, working 4 increase evenly spaced around each end of Oval. Join with slip stitch in first single crochet—112 single crochet. Fasten off B.

Round 10 With right side facing, join C in any single crochet, chain

1, single crochet in each single crochet around, working 4 increases evenly spaced around each end of Oval. Join with slip stitch in first single crochet—120 single crochet. Fasten off.

FILLER 1

Row 1 With right side facing and largest hook, with lower edge of Bottom Half on top, join C in first single crochet on bottom of gulley between Large Oval and Circle 1, chain 1, single crochet in each single crochet across bottom of gulley, slip stitch in next 2 single crochet on sloped edge of Circle 1. Turn.

Row 2 Single crochet in each single crochet across, single crochet in next single crochet on slope edge of Large Oval, slip stitch in next single crochet on slope. Turn.

Row 3 Single crochet in each single crochet across, single crochet in next single crochet on slope edge of Circle 1, slip stitch in next single crochet on slope. Turn.

Repeat Rows 2–3 until top edge of Filler is aligned with top edge of Large Oval side of Bottom Half, adjusting number of stitches as needed to keep work flat, ending with a right side row on Circle 1

side of Filler.

Next Row Single crochet in each single crochet across Filler 1, single crochet in each single crochet across edge of Bottom Half over Large Oval to last stitch before piece starts to curve down. Turn.

Next Row Chain 1, single crochet in each single crochet across to top of Circle 1, slip stitch in next 2 single crochet on slope. Turn.

Next Row Single crochet in each single crochet across. Fasten off C.

FILLER 2

Row 1 With right side facing and largest hook, with top edge of Bottom Half on top, join C in first single crochet on bottom of gulley between Circle 1 and Large Oval, chain 1, single crochet in each single crochet across bottom of gulley, slip stitch in next 2 single crochet on sloped edge of Large Oval. Turn.

Row 2 Single crochet in each single crochet across, single crochet in next single crochet on sloped edge of Circle 1, slip stitch in next single crochet on slope. Turn.

Row 3 Single crochet in each single crochet across, single crochet in next single crochet on sloped edge of Large Oval, slip stitch in next

single crochet on slope. Turn.

Repeat Rows 2–3 until top edge of Filler is aligned with top edge of Large Oval side of Bottom Half, adjusting number of stitches as needed to keep work flat, ending with a wrong side row on Circle 1 side of Filler.

Next Row Single crochet in each single crochet across Filler 2, single crochet in each single crochet across edge of bottom half over large oval to last stitch before piece starts to curve down. Turn.

Next Row Chain 1, single crochet in each single crochet across to top edge of Circle 1, single crochet in each of next 9 single crochet on top of Circle 1. Turn.

Work 3 rows even. Fasten off C.

ASSEMBLY

Place all pieces on a flat surface, following construction diagram for placement. With large-eyed, blunt needle and C, sew bottom edge of Circle 2 to first 7 stitches on top edge of Filler 2, sew bottom edge of Circle 3 to last 5 stitches of Filler 2, center Small Oval over remaining stitches on top edge of Filler 2 and sew in place, leaving a gap on either side.

FILLER 3

Row 1 With right side facing and largest hook, join C in first single crochet on slope of small oval above the space between small oval and Circle 3, skip first single crochet in gap, single crochet in next single crochet, single crochet in each single crochet across to 1 stitch before Circle 3, slip stitch in next single crochet on Circle 3, slip stitch in next single crochet on slope of Circle 3. Turn.

Row 2 Skip next single crochet, single crochet in each single crochet across to last single crochet, slip stitch in next 2 single crochet on slope of Small Oval. Turn.

Row 3 Skip next single crochet, single crochet in each single crochet across to last single crochet, slip stitch in next 2 single crochet on slope of circle 3. Turn.

Repeat Rows 2–3 until slopes are parallel, adjusting number of stitches as needed to keep work flat. Work even in pattern until slopes start to curve out. Continue to work rows of single crochet, increase on end of each row as for Filler 1, until top edge of Filler 3 aligns with top edges of small oval and Circle 3. Fasten off C.

FILLER 4

Row 1 With right side facing and largest hook, join C in first single crochet on slope of Circle 2 above the space between circle 2 and small oval. Skip first single crochet in gap, single crochet in next single crochet, single crochet in each single crochet across to 1 stitch before Small Oval, slip stitch in next single crochet on small oval, slip stitch in next single crochet on slope of Small Oval. Turn.

Work as for Filler 3 until top edge of Filler 4 is aligned with top edge of small oval.

Next Row Single crochet in each single crochet across Filler 4, single crochet in each single crochet across top edge of Small Oval and Filler 3, ending with slip stitch in next stitch on edge of Circle 3. Fasten off.

BORDER

Round 1 With wrong side facing and largest hook, join C in first free single crochet on edge of Large Oval (to the left of Filler 1). Slip stitch in each stitch around end of Large Oval, slip stitch in each stitch up side of Filler 2, slip stitch in each stitch around Circle 3, slip stitch in each stitch across top of Filler 4, slip stitch in each stitch around Circle 2, slip stitch in each stitch down side edge of Filler 2, slip stitch in each stitch around Circle 1 to beginning of Filler 1, double crochet in each stitch across last row of Filler 1. Join with slip stitch in first slip stitch. Fasten off. Weave in ends.

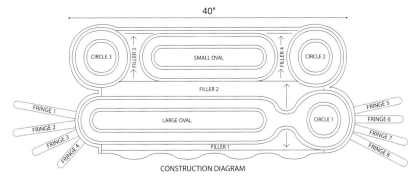

CONSTRUCTION DIAGRAM

YARN GLOSSARY

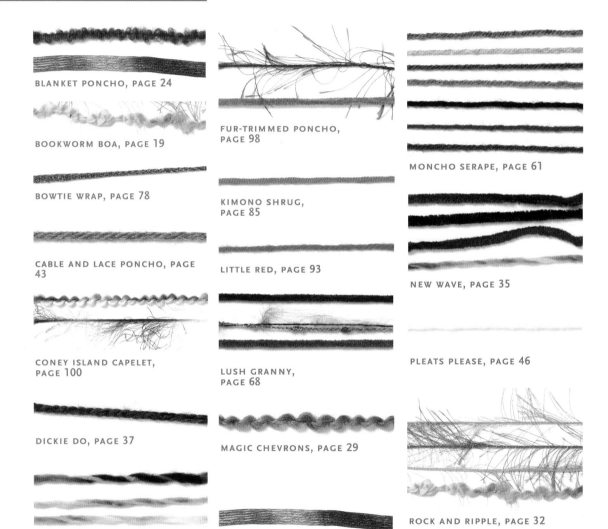

BLANKET PONCHO, PAGE 24

BOOKWORM BOA, PAGE 19

BOWTIE WRAP, PAGE 78

CABLE AND LACE PONCHO, PAGE 43

CONEY ISLAND CAPELET, PAGE 100

DICKIE DO, PAGE 37

THE FLAPPER, PAGE 54

FUR-TRIMMED PONCHO, PAGE 98

KIMONO SHRUG, PAGE 85

LITTLE RED, PAGE 93

LUSH GRANNY, PAGE 68

MAGIC CHEVRONS, PAGE 29

MESH PONCHO, PAGE 80

MONCHO SERAPE, PAGE 61

NEW WAVE, PAGE 35

PLEATS PLEASE, PAGE 46

ROCK AND RIPPLE, PAGE 32

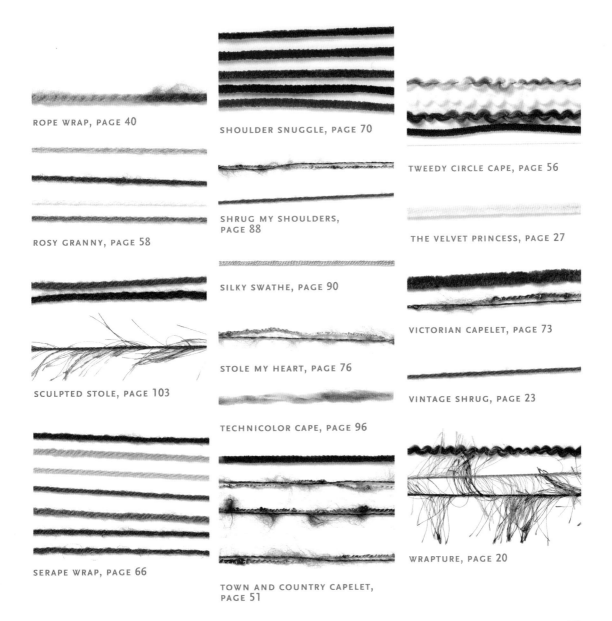

ROPE WRAP, PAGE 40

ROSY GRANNY, PAGE 58

SCULPTED STOLE, PAGE 103

SERAPE WRAP, PAGE 66

SHOULDER SNUGGLE, PAGE 70

SHRUG MY SHOULDERS, PAGE 88

SILKY SWATHE, PAGE 90

STOLE MY HEART, PAGE 76

TECHNICOLOR CAPE, PAGE 96

TOWN AND COUNTRY CAPELET, PAGE 51

TWEEDY CIRCLE CAPE, PAGE 56

THE VELVET PRINCESS, PAGE 27

VICTORIAN CAPELET, PAGE 73

VINTAGE SHRUG, PAGE 23

WRAPTURE, PAGE 20

INDEX